The Eyes Behind My Eyes

The Eyes Behind My Eyes

for Alex

PANTHER
PRESS

barbara leavell smith

ALSO BY BARBARA LEAVELL SMITH

The Windward and the Leeward Sides © 1974.

The Eyes Behind My Eyes is a work of fiction. Names, characters, places and incidents are the products of the author's imagination or are used fictitiously. Any resemblance to actual events, locales, or persons, living or dead, is entirely coincidental.

Copyright © 2014 by Barbara Leavell Smith
All rights reserved. No part of this book may be used or reproduced in any form, electronic or mechanical, including photocopying, recording, or scanning into any information storage and retrieval system, without written permission from the author except in the case of brief quotation embodied in critical articles and reviews.

Cover design by CarolLynn Langley
Cover art by Anna Fowler Bannon

Printed in the United States of America

The Troy Book Makers • Troy, New York • thetroybookmakers.com

To order additional copies of this title, contact your favorite local bookstore or visit www.tbmbooks.com and Amazon.com

ISBN: 978-1-61468-255-4

*I dedicate this book of poems to my children,
Anna, Sarah and Walt, with all my love.*

Thank You

—to my friends CarolLynn Langley for the cover photo and design, Penny Gebhard and Nicole Meyers Cejudo for help with typing poems.

—to my daughter, Anna Fowler Bannon, for the cover art and John Bannon for scanning documents and for technial support.

—and, especially, to my step-son Peter Anton Sjogren, for his many years of support and encouragement, for typing, retyping, filing and doing the yeoman's work of getting this book together. He has been my editor, my cheerleader and my great friend.

Contents

Two Moons

two moons	1
reunion	2
anna's dream (triolet)	3
what fishing is	4
santa claus lost	6
the robin's nest	7
to him that hath shall be given	8
the snowman	9
tidal pools	10
tidal pools (villanelle)	11
ballad of the weaver	12
the precious stone	13
beware of the irish faeries	14
1976	16
anna's house	17
after your graduation	18
love poem for my son's wife	19
moving to texas	20
journey of a lifetime	22

Humpty-Dumptedness Healers

to a friend	27
forever, for an hour	28
somewhere once	29
after the visit of an old friend	30
how to be a good lover	31
the other sermon	32
master dawdler	34
hospital visit	36
the home stretch	37
me and my dog	38

if he had had his way	39
elegy for panch	42
if only	44

The Figure In The Foreground

the figure in the foreground	49
the puppy	50
opening day	51
the hemlock tree	52
the sound of the waterfall	54
he loves me, he loves me not	55
the other	56
the fifth dimension	57
west wind	58
the other side of time	59
why the birds sing	61

Heros

camus and susuki	65
no room in the inn	66
evelyn flint	68
czelslavia (celia) bryke bailey	70
the zen of plumbing	72

Places

mont sainte victoire	77
market of provence (rondeau)	78
saint véran	79
cannes	80

proof 81
welch mountain 82
the salt marsh 84
you can't get here from there 86
alaska 87
voyage to the end of the world 88
the outgroup 93
my polish freighter 94
flight from paris 97

It's About This Flower

it's about this flower 103
the pilgrims 104
out out damn spot 105
let's boycott the war and go to the olympics 106
tug of war 107
the florida recount 108
tsunami 2005 110
another kind of flag 111
the way out 112
revelations 113
stars, asters and other lighthouses 114

Cranberry Lake

the cardinal flowers 119
sleight of cloud 120
cathedral window 121
indian summer 122
inspiration 123
visitor 124
days 125
forever and a day 126
eternity has time 127
opening camp duet 128

summer home	129
red geraniums	130
putting away summer	132
the buoy light	133
his canoe	134
pilgrimage to the source	136

Belle Isle

leeward and windward	141
côte sauvage	142
port andro	143
sauzon	144
island in the sea	146
wanderfreund	148

Night Work

night work	153
perennials	154
the heroine	155
shadow liberation	156
moonlighting	157
my apartment in paris	158
the far room	160

Seasons

miracles	165
diary	166
inheriting winter	167
january thaw	168
march	169
may	170
june	171
let september come (ballade)	172
a song for november	173

Glimpses

two roads	177
clear days	178
red	179
the bright side	180
eureka	181
the truth about roses	182
afloat but not adrift	183
distant harvest	184
the dog star	185
souvenirs	186
habit	187
the source	188
airport	189
the chicken or the egg	190
traitor	191
recipe for enriched bread	192

Happily Ever After

diamond	207
how i do love thee	208
forgiveness	209
the way to the bridge	210
time machine?	211
hunter's moon	212
ghosts	213
remodeling	214
the stowaways	216
out of season	217
pastorale	218
how to sail in one easy lesson	219
october snowstorm	220
the sunflower	221

the guest	222
pass words	223
born again, and again	224
but these candles	225
the difference	226
if winter comes	228
departures	229
love story	230
his daylillies	231
chill draft	232
tryst	233
physics lesson	234
object lesson	236
secret passages	237
new friends	238
that number has been disconnected	240
the next lover	241
once upon a time	242

Questions

bitten moon	247
depending on which world you mean	248
where the lilacs are	249
the miracle	250
self portrait	251
not you	252
frontiers	253
coming across my old wedding portrait	254
my old child	255

Answers

my old child — ii	259
traveling light	260

nauset beach	261
look, ma, no hands!	263
transubstantiation	264
altars and fountains	265
meaning	266
thanks giving	267
i am that i am that i am	268
after the breakfast dishes	269
a fool's paradise	271
something more	272
what if she forgot to leave her glass slipper?	273
how to break a spell	275
the hills and the path (sestina)	277
afterlife	279
mary and martha	280
how to shovel the walk	281
all natural	282
the intruder	283
just say yes	285
clearings	286
town and mountains	287
the girl in the white robe	288

Endangered Species

I have something
strong and fragile
as a tiny pink flower
on a mountain top,
rare as a scarlet tanager,
glimpsed once through branches...
Be careful where you step.

If there would be
a violin playing on a battlefield
or a rose opening in the snow
or a clear corner
in my cluttered house,
that would be it.
   Sshhh...

How The Clearing Became Clear

This summer you won't be coming back,
not feeling up to it.
So what should we do on the island while we are there?
"Well, paint the dock — to make it last,
varnish the oars — to make them last,
build a seawall — to make the island last,
and yes, if you can, keep the clearing open
on the east end of the island.
I think that there should be a clearing there."

You had made that clearing
years ago
I knew.
Now I know
you had meant that clearing
too.

This summer I have come back
and missed you here, everywhere.
But wandering to the clearing am surprised
to find you, and it, with the eyes behind my eyes.

Yes, there will always be a clearing there.

Two Moons

two moons

Years ago
I took you from your toys to see the moon
you did not know.

Then yesterday
you took me from my toils to see the moon.
I'd lost the way.

So now
we have two moons —
the one I gave you years ago
and the one you gave me yesterday.

reunion

This was the time of our own,
staying on at the island alone
after summer and before September.

No one to know we were here,
the fifty-third week of the year
after summer and before September.

Breakfasts by our morning stove,
evenings by our fire,
and the late crystal sun at noon
in our island cove.

We saw the lake the morning it was born,
we heard the loon before men came to hear,
we paddled in the rivers of the beaver,
we passed along the pathways of the deer.

But in your little boat, you look
ridiculously tall,
the jacket in your closet here
seems absurdly small.

And now you tell of flights beyond the clouds
and lands I only dreamed that you know well,
and dreams I never dreamed.
And there are journeys that you do not tell.

These are those same whole days,
but we go home separate ways
after summer and before September.

anna's dream (triolet)

A princess marrying a prince
and gaining life forever green,
you dreamt last night was you, convinced
a princess marrying a prince
can be. Ah, it's a long time since
the last night I could dream of being
a princess marrying a prince
and gaining life forever green!

what fishing is

We had both looked forward to it.
Getting up early before the others,
an extra sweater, tiptoes and shivers,
coffee and the cold stove in the checkered kitchen,
cereal for you poured in a bowl, half eaten.
Mist footless across the water, and five horse motor
cutting fresh tracks through smoothness and through silence
to the pool, inlet of the lake,
part and set apart.
There I took you fishing your first time.

Dirt on fingers and worms on hooks
lines thrown over the side and pulled out to the right length
we waited.
Was that what fishing was?
Getting up early in the morning, to wait?
Coming to the source of the lake, to wait?

Your line went taut!
It tightened you, half pulled half pulling
and roller coaster white
caught —
more than the fish,.

Let that one be the one that got away.
Here, I'll help bait your hook —
No, you said
outside the cubes and spheres of my understanding.
Afraid of losing it again? Tired of the game?
(But you were calm now, let down
or let up, earthward.)
Afraid more . . .
of catching what you'd waited for!

That place I'd known and fishing I'd known and you,
but not you-fishing-there.
It has been years since then.

But that time remains as one shape of understanding
able to hold — in you, or me,
that sudden halt of the headlong heart
that would not grasp the grail for cup.

santa claus lost

You'll grant it's true —
now in August, gladly.
At six, a person's got to know the score.
It seems more gain than loss,
at first, to get the facts.
Besides, you'd had your doubts before.

After all, you weren't born yesterday.
But, ah! When Christmas comes,
and bells and stars and snow,
and with them your old habit of believing?
— Then will you play both sides,
for all you know.

the robin's nest

We could hardly believe they'd been so bold
or so foolhardy as to build
their nest right on the fence. It showed
too much until the fence-vine filled

with leaves. The first day it was found,
we didn't dare hope they wouldn't discover
their mistake, once they'd looked around,
and go away to build another.

There was something tenderly strong about it:
the way a seedling splits a stone,
It mattered. We hadn't missed it, without it,
but now we would, if they were gone.

We did the best we could, going
the long way round their privacy,
telling no one, and not mowing.
But it was more formality

than anything, and from despair
more than from faith.
                              We waited a week.
Then, thinking we did not care,
we risked that quick and casual peek —

I had been told, but never knew
till then that robins' eggs are blue!

to him that hath shall be given

The quince bush is in bloom again. Watch soon
the oriole will come, he always does.
I can't remember just the way it was
last spring, whether he came because she bloomed
or she bloomed because he came. It's hard to guess,
they happen so at once. That thrill of gold
around the branches! It's him, the oriole
come back, flashing a glint of God, to bless.

O glory, glory, glory, radiant bush,
what need have you of such a golden rush
of wings? Are you not crowned enough?

Yet which came first I have not seen,
The coronation or the queen.

the snowman

One day there was such a big snowstorm
that they closed work and school.
The man hurried home
to do something very important.
So did the boy.
When I caught up to them,
the man was shoveling the driveway,
and the boy was building a snowman.

Of course the driveway has to be shoveled.
Otherwise you couldn't get out
to go places and do things
or in case of emergency.
You would have to stay home
and do nothing,
and take your chances.

But
after the driveways are all shoveled,
will there be time enough
to build your snowman?

tidal pools

The tide has gone like autumn from the trees,
the tide has gone
out of the bay in rivers,
down from the rocks in waterfalls,
but slowly,
so that we do not know its going,
only that it has gone.

As autumn dying from the trees
gives birth to branches and distant hills,
the tide has gone,
delivering rocks and beaches
and a scene always as new as sunrise
on their age-old stage.

And they come now, the ones that know —
gulls scouting the scroll of froth,
and children with hands on their knees,
hearts coasting like hawks . . .

children sitting together at silent altars,
watching,
watching the robe hem of the tide
take up their solemn offering —
transfusions of themselves into the sea . . .

children like you,
in childhood's windless wandering afternoon,
watching,
watching the universe of a tidal pool,
after the tide has gone.

tidal pools (villanelle)

They still explore those rocks beside the sea
in childhood's long and drifting summer day,
though you have not been back there, you and she,

since that last time. Then it came clear to me,
watching you there the way you used to play,
they still explore those rocks beside the sea,

they still invent the afternoon, and see
a universe in tidal pools today,
though you have not been back there, you and she.

As your offerings to the tide wash presently
to other children in some distant bay,
they still explore those rocks beside the sea.

Though now you each keep different company,
have separate dreams, go home a separate way,
though you have not been back there, you and she,

they sit together watching silently,
or, secret in their moonlight holiday,
they still explore those rocks beside the sea.

The tide has gone like autumn from the tree,
but tidal pools, like leaves near streetlamps, stay.
They still explore those rocks beside the sea,
though you have not been back there, you and she.

ballad of the weaver

Mother, mother can you tell
why you work an evening,
what besides the shuttled strand
is woven in your weaving?

Mother, since your child has grown,
why, instead of grieving,
have you given to your hands
this new work of weaving?

Once his hunger met my breast,
each the one relieving;
now, when fullness swells to pain,
I weave it in my weaving.

Once his crying met my arms,
each the other needing;
rest, return and tenderness
are woven in my weaving.

I would be God and part the sea!
But he will find in living
a way for him. We both are free
by my wise art of weaving.

the precious stone

The sea was a child's scene
a dark bright blue surprise
white sands and light blue skies —

The day was a child's dream
hot sun and blowing wind
and high surf rolling in —

And the wet stones
were jewels.

We watched in the salt marsh,
we walked behind the dunes
on our fine afternoon

Dear truce in our lives rush,
a place to walk together
on a day of forever —

And we picked up
one stone.

Yesterday, at the bottom of my pocket,
I came across the stone

and all the sea and all the sand and sky
the sun and surf and all the blowing wind
and all we said and felt there you and I
was mine again!

beware of the irish faeries

I want to say to that woman on the bench
with her little boy beside her,
arms around her neck,
whispering in her ear

I want to say "Oh
hold him listen to him don't
read the paper don't
look in the mirror."

I want to tell her to hold to listen to feel to
walk hand in hand looking at leaves to
sit on steps together eating picnics to
read his favorite book about tractors
the same book every night,
knowing his warmth on her lap.

I want to say to her, "Listen
to him wanting to tell you everything,
listen and listen and listen.
See his whole laughter on the swing."

I want to tell her to tuck him in,
so slowly,
as he tells her his thoughts of the day, and
to leave the door open a crack.

Or else one day,
when it is too late,
she will be sorting out an old trunk
and come across a blue sailor cap
much too small
then she will run to all the rooms
call run look here there
she will call run look ask
ask his sisters his dog his picture ask
all but his tall namesake
sleeping in his bed.

And know, too late,
that he is gone without goodbye,
leaving no forwarding address.

1976

I've kept it.
Brought it along through the moves
when most things got thrown out,
that little flag, with the circle of thirteen stars,
you bought for me at our town parade
on the bicentennial of the fourth of July.

Your sisters were gone on a glee club trip,
and I had some idea I could get away
without celebrating that year,
and catch up on things.
Not you.
I guess the flag was a thank you.

I have forgotten all the thousand thousand days
of catching up on things,
but not that day.
We had red, white and blue
breakfast, lunch and supper,
watched the fourth of July come
around the world on TV,
went to the parade, a fair,
a band concert and a bonfire
together.

And I loved your delight,
which has always been
maybe my favorite thing
in the world.
Forced into it by love,
I climbed another rung of joy that day.

anna's house

In Anna's house, stars illuminate
the ceiling when the dark turns on,
soft leaves
and grasses fountain from the floors,
sweet wreathes
of tangled herbs and ribbons coronate
each jutting thing,
flames fascinate
on magic Christmas trees,
and rainbows radiate
from crystals in the sun, like fantasies.

One room,
at the top of the stairs, is empty.
With a white rug and four tall candles,
it is as clear as Chartres.

And yes, the clearness of it interweaves
in all the rooms with fine complexities
of decoration,
as though they were the warp and weft
of celebration.

after your graduation

That cartoon caterpillar
dropped from a beech beside the August trail
had thrilled us being so theatrical
great and bright and green with great brown spots,
and so we'd brought it home
wrapped in the leaf it might have fallen from
and put it in a jar, so it had put itself
in a cocoon.

We had forgot about it.

One day, on the kitchen floor,
I almost swept a resting moth,
a kind we'd never seen beside the lake,
a moth of dreams and of the moon —
great and pale and gray with great brown spots . . .

Yes, there was a hole in the cocoon!

The day you walked away into your life,
your back was that hole again.

Godspeed the moth!

love poem for my son's wife

Maybe, when he was that little boy
sitting on the steps with me
wondering about things . . .
you were a little girl
walking in your garden
dreaming of a someday prince . . .

I know, since I came across
his old sailor cap,
grown too small,
I have been waiting for you . . .

I didn't know, though, that
once you found him,
I would too.

I didn't know, either, that
you would be no someday princess,
but a real woman, one of my own kind,
with deep eyes and clear voice,
telling me new things in an old language.

I didn't know that,
once he found you,
I would too.

moving to texas

That's a good sign! There he is already
down packing the U-Haul truck.
Well then,
things must be clearing out up there.
But no, there it still all is —
and she wading vaguely here and there
like a Red Cross worker in a disaster area
when it is too late to save survivors.

In the kitchen, a friend who's volunteered an hour,
heroically packs dishes.
Other friends busy up and down the stairs,
check on how things are going,
scratch their heads,
beach comb for clear tasks,
make jokes, drink coffee, struggle
against the opium of despair.

It may be that they see the shape of things,
he and she, but as for us, the friends and I,
we labor blindly out of love.
Only some mindless faith in happy endings
can picture the two of them, and the dog,
settled triumphantly in the truck cab the next day,
can picture the apartment empty, swept clean,
remembering them secretly in its walls.

Well, they didn't leave the next day,
but the day after they did.
Happy endings often take an extra day.
The friends and I had to ship some boxes,
tend to some odds and ends.
More than they'd planned had to be
given away or left behind or put out with the trash.

But one man's trash is
the young couple, just moving into town,
tying the mattress on top of their car,
the girl from the pizza parlor next door
taking all the plants no one else wanted,
the woman with her baby in a backpack
fishing out the curtain rods,
the Italian bag lady returning the bottles,
the trash men, themselves, picking out a photo that they liked.

I walk through the empty apartment, swept clean,
remembering them secretly in its walls.
I have been here before in other lives.
This new clear opening of empty rooms and
A truck on its way to Texas
is an old station of the human heart.

As I lock the door, leaving the key for the next tenant,
a flock of geese is headed south, too.

journey of a lifetime

Not everyone, after a lifetime,
can go back across an ocean
to the country of your first loves,
but everyone has a country.

Everyone has a place, too,
the trailhead of your life,
like that exit of the metro
onto Boulevard St. Michel,

and old friends from that time
when you gave each other *The Prophet* and the poems of Rilke,
and stood together at the back
through all six Brandenburg Concertos.

not everyone can travel
to the Seine at sunrise after a sleepless night,
to Montmartre in love and *La Vie en Rose,*
but everyone has a sunrise, and everyone has a song.

So you would know the completeness
if your daughter, now with sunrises of her own,
could come back with you across an ocean,
could stand with you on a bridge across the Seine,

could speak with your old friends
in their own language,
search with you for a certain window
and a boat with yellow sails.

And you would know the sweet sweetness
if your son, now with songs of his own,
could walk out with you along the cliff
where you walked on that first day,

could stand beside you on the ferry,
watching a certain island disappear,
remembering, for himself now, its long June sunsets,
glimpsing that dream-pulled girl of sixty years ago,

and if you could talk with them there
the way you talked with those old friends,
about love with her over wine in a café,
about God with him on a path beside the sea.

Humpty-Dumptedness Healers

to a friend

The loitering, limp bums
of my soul, being scattered
and at odds, dread even you,
especially you.

And then, with your old need you come
and do
what all the king's horses and all the king's men
could never do.

forever, for an hour

At the hearth of your friendship
I warm my November chill.

In the clearing of your smile
I look up and see the sky.

In the wholeness of your song
I live forever, for an hour.

somewhere once

There was a time
when there were whole afternoons,
when waves stretched on the pebbled beach
and days were meadows.

We walked down the long fragrant hill
with our tin buckets
and collected shapes of colored glass
and lucky stones.

There was a place
where summer grew like the corn,
where lamplight soft on the warm walls
tucked us to sleep.

We played house in our private grove
and paper dolls on rainy afternoons.
Summer belonged to us
and the wind blew in our hair.

after the visit of an old friend

You know how moods of weather come
like a lost country we've misplaced
(but whose language comes back to us),
as, after days of up and at 'em sun,
soft rain,
or after hours of blind and closed in storm,
the stars.

So when you'd come and gone, old friend,
clear sweet softness stayed behind —
presence
of far remembered weather
those spendthrift years of world enough and time
that only could be found together.

how to be a good lover

You are eight and I am eighty,
and we know a thing or two,
like the wowness
of seeing each other again.
You pride yourself on being smart at math,
but there is something you are smarter at.

You know how to tell me, without my asking,
(because how would I know to ask?)
what it felt like to finally
be able to count to a hundred.

You know how to ask me, without my telling,
(because how would I know to tell?)
"What are you afraid of?
Not just what everyone is afraid of,
like storms and bears,
but just you,
like I am afraid of the dark,
a little, or at least I used to be."

And you know how to leave the others
at video games, saying,
"Let's go play together now.
I can have video games any day,
but not you."

the other sermon

We were having a love affair,
my little granddaughter and I.
Sunday morning we went to church
and sat together in the front pew,
because Mommy and Daddy sing in the choir.
After the children's talk
we took her little brother to his room downstairs.
We were going to come back up,
and she was going to sit ever so quietly.

But she wanted to take me further down
to show me a "scary place". It wasn't far.
She knew that. I didn't.
I said no, we would go later,
because I wanted to go back to church
and hear Mommy and Daddy sing the anthem.
She insisted, I insisted back, and, after a little of that,
I said, firmly, she could come up with me now,
or stay down there with the other children.

I wanted her to be able to trust me
when I said no or yes
the way her Daddy could.
But she started back up in a huff
and straight she went
right into the choir
and into his warm arms.
Playing one against the other,
I thought, as children will.

No sense to follow her there
and make a spectacle
for the whole congregation.
I went to sit alone in my front pew —
fat and old and useless,
traitor to my son's trust.
And I had missed the choir's anthem,
with that joy of sitting back and being proud.
I busied myself with empty rituals.

And then, suddenly,
he was sitting there with me in my pew,
still holding her encircled,
singing the hymn with me
in that sweet true baritone of his.
And then, suddenly,
he had passed her —
with one clear move,
into my unsuspecting, but familiar arms,

healing our love affair
and my uselessness
and the lost anthem,
healing even the long emptiness
since that little boy of thirty years ago
outgrew my lap.

Warm arms are the only answer
to the hard questions.

master dawdler

You have a true vocation for it, you
are called.
All my focuspleases and hurryups and payattentionnows are
blah blah blah.
But you are paying attention
to that water spider you're experimenting with
(though one might think you're just tormenting it)
to that slug you're scientifically observing
(though one might think this is just a delaying tactic)
to why
the light goes on when you open the restroom door
to all the other things you can do with
a marshmallow
a long fork
a campfire.

You have a passion for it, you
have to do it, you
get pulled back to it when,
out of love or pity or sheer duress
you have interrupted it
to set the table or pick up your stuff or brush your teeth or whatever
seems to be so important to me or to the survival of mankind.
It is bigger than you are, you
just can't help yourself.

Once, when, for an afternoon,
I let you be my teacher,
then
all that I've been searching for, through meditation and yoga and
Tai Chi and hypnosis and massage therapy and selfhelp books and
all
those famous alpha waves and low blood pressure and low cholesterol and
presence
here
now
I have been trying to find
found me.

hospital visit

Goodbye, my morning field of goldenrod,
Goodbye, my chapel of trees,
Goodbye, my tree-mess.

I have to leave now,
have to take the turnpike to the hospital in Boston,
have to go where only Bostonians know the way.

Shield me, my warrior armor,
Gird me, my black belt,
Arm me, my breath of fire.

I have to storm these huge swinging doors,
Have to brave this potted palm lobby,
Have to slough through to the glass elevators.

Warm me, half smiles of strangers,
Lull me, workaday orderlies,
Hearten me, boy with a balloon.

I have to walk past all the hospital rooms of my life,
Have to fend through a world in black and white,
Have to be nobody, nowhere.

Stead me, my voyager staff,
Dull me, my numbness cloak,
Aim me, my bow of will.

Hello, there in 612-A, dear technicolor you,
Hello, dear Red Sox fan, dear lover of loons,
Hello, dear somebody.

the home stretch

There would be a long hill, more like
a sloping field, full of long grass
and of course sun and shining, because
everything would be open that has been closed —
like the paths to the past,
and like the long sloping shining field to you.

And I would be standing there on the hill, and
then — across a field of long grass, and maybe
daisies — seeing you, knowing you.
(You had been waiting.) And then —
overflowing with all these
waiting for your praises
triumphs, and with these aches waiting
for your arms, and then
I would begin to run to you.

Oh, I can feel that rippling shining running
overflowing,
the heart running more than the feet,
with all the half-laughed, half-cried crowding running
through a long hill to be complete,
all-laughed, all-cried.
I do not picture it ending.

me and my dog

Sometimes I wonder why
he wants me to go with him.
You could hardly say
that we walk together.

He follows every scent and sound
on both sides of the path at once,
disappears ahead, turns up behind,
leaping through underbrush like a deer —
comes back to see what's taking me so long,
stands watching, head cocked
with much love, but no understanding,
as I pick my way over a patch of ice,
then canters off his gay lop-sided gait,
tail like a plume and ears like flowing hair.

You could hardly say
that we walk together . . .
and yet, more than anything,
he wants me to go with him.

if he had had his way

we would have put aside
all those dull incomprehensible occupations of ours,
to devote ourselves utterly
to the care and feeding of him —
to letting him in and letting him out, for example.
After all, whenever caninely possible,
he took care of that matter himself —
jumping open swinging doors,
nosing open doors that weren't quite closed,
bounding through screen doors with no problems,
to him.
We had to understand that his purpose in life
was to keep track of things — of passing
dogs, cats, rabbits, woodchucks, horses and motorcycles —
real or imagined,
and, especially of us.
Our every move was a potential threat or joy.

If he had had his way,
we would have always stayed
both of us securely sitting down, up to no mischief,
at noon beside the brook in summer sun,
or lamplit evenings by our winter stove.
Then he could lie down at last,
stretch luxuriously all four legs at once,
heave a great sigh,
and sleep his martyred sleep.

if he had his way cont.

If he had had his way,
when we did get up,
it would have always been to take him for a walk
(though there was some question as to who took whom).
He'd bark and scold us to the door,
firecrackering in all directions,
pivot and pirouette and leap and slide,
then dash outside.
He'd even leave a chance to eat,
We tried him once on that —
he did think twice, but still he came.

The trouble with eating was,
with him, it was over so soon —
all anticipation, no savoring, no gourmet.
But still he was a slave to it.
He'd stand there, covering our every move
like a basketball guard —
ears pricked, head cocked, tail
encouraging us with its potential waving.
If he had had his way,
our first thought would have been
to find 'a little something' just for him —
the whole pork roast would be fine, thank you,
to begin with.

And, if he had had his way,
we would have devoted ourselves utterly
to petting and praising him
as he pranced up and down, up and down,
high-stepping, fine and noble
as the drum major of a marching band,
but so silly, with a pillow in his mouth.

If he had had his way,
we would have always been there
to protect him from thunderstorms
that, without a doubt, had it in for him
personally and in particular,
to pull out his porcupine quills,
and, after nights of the full moon,
to bind up the wounds of the old warrior-lover,
when nature let him go, and he dragged home.

Muscled and slim at thirteen years,
aging with dignity just by growing deaf
and sleeping most of the time,
there was another side of him, though,
that didn't need us,
that had better things to do —
his daily rounds about the neighborhood,
the chase of cats and rabbits and falling leaves,
and, best of all,
tracking and side-tracking in his beloved woods.
It seemed he could go on forever there,
At home as blind men in the dark.

We would have left the world behind,
Filled up our packs with roasts of pork,
And followed him through endless pathless woods,

If he had had his way.

elegy for panch

Wild-eyed, ears flat, his instinct jammed
by pavement, whizzing cars — no one
to ask the way, no one to know ...
while I all night awake to dreams
of barking at the door, and run
to meet black shadows on the snow ...
He does not come.

Dull thud, skull crushed, black body still —
his frantic journey done,
slapped down and pushed aside.
While I all day search other roads,
and seem at last to come upon
his spirit bounding through the woods ...
He will not come.

If I had only been a child enough
to dream that he could roam
so far, to follow one wild clue,
I might have come upon him there,
I might have brought him home —
if I had searched the whole night through ...
He does not come.

Each morning when he heard me stir,
rejoicing that the day'd begun,
he'd always come beside my bed
for me to hug and pet and scratch.
He'd stretch, then lick me with his tongue,
and burrow down his big black head . . .
But he does not come.

He slept a lot as he grew old,
but never once passed up the fun
of coming for a walk. He'd bark
and twirl, beside himself with joy —
slow motion body almost young,
possessed by full speed puppy heart . . .
And he does not come.

And now, day after day, the step
outside the door stays stubborn stone,
no matter if I go to see
again. And now, day after day,
the empty road winds its way home,
the empty fields lie changelessly . . .
He does not come and he does not come
and he does not come.

if only

If I had only known where he was
trying to come home the wrong way,
wild-eyed, ears flat, tongue
hanging to the side — like other dogs
I've seen on highways —
careening rudderless,
once instinct jammed
by pavement, headlights, whizzing cars,
with no road map, no thought to ask the way . . .

If I had only been a child enough
to quit the busywork of reason,
the search near home in likely places,
in daylight, between meals,
with methodical despair . . .
If I had only been a child enough
to look all night
on roads you'd never think of,
tears burning my eyes, my shoulders set,
to follow maybe one wild crazy clue,
to go and go,
not let them call me back — a child enough to hope . . .

Then I might have come upon him
by the road there,
might have been hardly able — just for
a second — to believe it was him,
so far away.
He, though would not have been at all
surprised that I had come —
I always had. He would have been glad
to get in the car, the nightmare over,
and go home . . .

And you'd have been so pleased and so amazed
to hear us at the door, and see him come,
put his head down beside your knee
the way he does,
look in his dish,
drink a long drink of water,
and find his bed under the piano.
We would have sat down then, and
told the amazing story of how I found him.
And, after awhile, you would have
gone back to reading your book,
and I to cooking supper,
while he, too tired that night to be enticed by smells,
slept in his bed —
the three of us, beside our winter stove.

The Figure In The Foreground

the figure in the foreground

Bird breaking
sky, boat making
sea buoyant,
birch in pine,
branch's line
measuring meadow behind,
paddle scrape
on still lake
sounding silence.

Grass and sky and green
and sea are only seen
by birch and branch and bird,
and silence only heard
by paddle's scrape.

So love makes landscape
of my life, since you are found,
shaping it one and whole and round.

the puppy

The puppy brings things
to lay at my feet —
a chewed-on rained-on teddy bear,
a dead blue jay, an anything —
"Here, because . . . well, I just brought them . . ."

So here
here is the shining planet
and here the way it feels to climb a mountain
and be crowned with the valley,
and here is yesterday's sunset
and last year's early autumn branch
and today's sudden breeze
and —

Here, because . . . well,
because I bring them
is how I know I love you.

opening day

I see now that the sun rehearsed its warmth
behind a cold wind curtain,
I see now that those birds I saw arrive,
too early, I was certain,
were waiting in the wings to take their cue,
and that those days of snow
were smuggling in what soon would fill the streams.
There was no way to know
that in the night the stage was set and all
the cast was placed in pose,
but when the sun arrived upon the scene
with dawn, the curtain rose.

You were not here to see and so I went
to tell it all to you,
how spring had come today, and you replied,
"Yes, I saw it too."

the hemlock tree

The hemlock tree stood in the angle
where our road left the one going deeper on
into the woods. Alone straight and dark
and evergreen above gray tangles of
deciduous branches and in front of them,
it had absorbed a thousand turnings homeward:
homeward with a sigh from wonderland,
homeward with relief from hell, or just
home from the store. It was the last milestone,
the one of almost there, the real reward
of every journey back, the unknown goal
of every going out.

That spring they were putting up new houses
along the road, the one going deeper on
into the woods, which eventually entailed
the continuation of the electric line
beyond our turn-off, that had been the end
of it before.
          That afternoon that spring
you came in early. I was washing the dishes —
you don't forget what you were doing: it fixes,
becomes forever the shape of feeling. You said,
"They cut down the hemlock."
                         That was the first
time we had spoken of it to each other,
or even to ourselves. It's not those things
we're conscious of that count as much as those
we take for granted.
               "Putting in new posts and clearing
the way for the power line up to the new houses."
"You let them?"

     "I didn't even know until
I saw it done. They could have left it there.
They didn't have to cut it. I'd thought they wouldn't."

You stood looking out the window, not at the tree,
we couldn't see it from the house. At nothing.

"Well, back to work," you sighed.
          "I'd make them pay."
"They knew I was upset, and said they'd saw
the tree for lumber we can use to build
a new roof for the barn."
         "I'd make them pay,
though, something, too. They should do more than that."

"What's the use? You know there's no way they could do
enough. It's not a toy that can be glued
back up."

  And you went back to work, and I
to washing dishes, saving my secret unbelief
yet awhile. Later I went to see,
expecting what could not be true would not
be true.

  I saw they had cut down the hemlock.

the sound of the waterfall

I used to wonder if a waterfall
made sound when no one heard
or if the strivings of a bird
were song
when no one came along.

But I could never get there first to see
since I could never get ahead of me.

But I don't wonder if my loveliness
before your love was such
or if, before your sculptor's touch,
my soul
or skin or tongue were whole.

Without you
sound or song or loveliness can't be —
I know ...

for I was here ahead of you to see.

he loves me,
he loves me not

I thought you'd be like him . . .
we walked a path together,
stood by a river,
strolled a summer
day of golden weather —
and made them more
because we passed together.
He gave me love,
and made me free
from me.

I thought you'd be like him . . .
but you stood your ground,
and let the river,
and let the summer
day be what we found
them, what they were —
and made me stand my ground.
You gave back me,
and made me free
from love.

the other

Stranger, stay stranger, but stay
here face to face
for we have far to come and far to go
before we meet, and all the distance
is a dance.
Stay near
stay stranger, but stay here.

>On one hill, one dark noon
>they say that one saved all
>others . . .
>Is the grail the rainbow going round
>and not the buried gold, at all?

Stranger, stay stranger, but stay
here long enough
not to discover, but to move together,
finding each other in the figure
of a dance.
Be dear
but stranger, and be here.

>In this hour, in this room
>come far enough to find
>one other . . .
>Oh, we have drunk a common wine!
>All are found if you are found.

the fifth dimension

Maybe you think it's just for you
that I've been singing
each new song for you
that I've been bringing
you to things and things to you.

Maybe you think it's just for you
that I've been playing
each old tune for you,
that I've been saying
tales and times and dreams to you.

Maybe you think it's just for you that I've been showing
all that's dear or old or new
to me, to you . . .

But partly it's a game I play
without your knowing,
since what I came upon one day
when you had come and gone again,
I looked at things I'd shown
to you
and saw what you had done
to them,
without your knowing.

west wind

An out of shape Atlas
trying to hold
a Humpty-Dumpty world,
a cross-eyed juggler
trying to catch
too many fallen sparrows
the boy who cried wolf
trying to cry
Wolf,
a Henny-Penny prophet
with ten tel-
ephones trying to tell
that the sky really is falling . . .

but the letter in my mailbox,
electric and alive,
blows a soft wind of summer,
a lost wind of summer,
opens wishing wells in May,
and grows daisies in a day.

Now — even if the world ends —
I won't believe it.

the other side of time

I was not looking for you there,
from forty years ago,
paddling like that along the shore
and calling to me through the woods
from the water down below.

I was not looking for you there,
for I had come alone,
come like some Rip Van Winkle ghost
to find forgotten or grown old
the people I had known.

I had made friends with solitude,
the wilderness in me —
arthritic, but that same old heart,
same voyager against the wind,
same sister to the tree.

I'd played the old victrola here,
those sentimental themes
of love that makes the world go round.
I'd seen a young girl dreaming, but
I could not see her dreams.

I didn't call you, but you came,
a Rip Van Winkle, too —
arthritic, too, but still with heart,
remembering how it used to be,
knowing the things I knew —

that world of forty years ago,
the inboard boats for hire,
the wooden bridge across the cove,
old timers and the tales they told,
the singing round the fire.

the other side of time cont.

>We are not strangers any more
>in a land we used to own,
>but royalty of Camelot,
>our kingdom come — both young and old,
>and neither young nor old.

>And now I'm looking for you there,
>though you cannot come, I know,
>paddling like that along the shore
>and calling to me through the woods
>from the water down below.

>I'll picnic in the sun all day,
>just knowing that you came,
>and then, because you've gone away,
>the next day and the next I'll sit
>inside and watch the rain.

>Then I'll walk a little taller, and
>my drudging chores be done
>to a song of somewhere violins,
>and lit by gold-washed colors, like
>the late hours of the sun.

>I'll see at the last that young girl's dream
>from forty years ago —
>that someone would come paddling there
>and calling to her through the woods
>from the water down below.

why the birds sing

I used to sing for sadness,
to spread it out to dry,
or bottle some of gladness
before its grapes went by.

I used to sing to name
some thing that flew — so high,
or play an ugly pain
into a lovely sigh.

Part to keep for tomorrow,
partly to calm the past,
from strands of joy and sorrow,
a pattern sung to last.

Then came you and love along,
a better music bringing —
I used to sing for song,
but now I sing for singing.

Heros

camus and susuki

You, doctor, fighting the plague in the city of Oran —
you, journalist, fighting the Nazis in the French underground,
fighting injustice and ignorance, fighting death —
you, man of struggle and caring,
of holding on —
you man for men,
yet loving the beaches, the trees, the sun.

And you monk, living in the mountains —
you, teacher, tending the fields, watching the hills,
walking — you, master, making tea, tasting —
you man of peace and prayer,
of letting go —
you man for the god in man,
yet finding it in the beaches, the trees, the sun.

You, daisy, cornflower, dandelion
between mowing, around rocks, through cracks —
and you stem, stamen, pistil, petal — flower.

Branches and roots, blood vessels, coral fans,
tidemarks in the sand,
rivers to the sea
heartbeats, drumbeats, clocks,
tides, loneliness and love,
breathing, waves —
and the pattern, the rhythm.

Skin walls
and the salt of old seas in our blood.

The me that meets you —
the I that is you.

no room in the inn

It had snowed all night; my car wouldn't
start; I had called the mechanic.
But the Priest was coming
so I had tried to tell the mechanic not to
come between 2 and 4 about unless there
was no other way but please to be sure and
come only not during that time when the
Priest was supposed to be there if he
could possibly manage it . . .

The Priest was coming to talk to me about
God and the Bible and My Soul.
The car had to be fixed because later I had to go out.
But I did hope we wouldn't be interrupted
at a time like that
by something like that.

The Priest came and, after all, we were not interrupted.
We talked about God for two hours.
But I was angry at the Priest and he was angry at me
and we didn't talk about that, because
that doesn't happen between a Priest and a Believer.

We talked about God
but God wasn't there.
The Priest left, and for an hour
God wasn't anywhere.

Then the mechanic came.
I didn't want to go out in the cold to meet him.
Having to get a car started in winter was a bore.

But Something skipped in me as I came down the stairs
and Something smiled in me and smiled at him
and the cold stayed outside me on the skin.

He was tired, clearly had been out all day
starting cars that wouldn't start
for cold, cranky people in a hurry.
I didn't think he could start mine.
We'd tried everything.

But he pulled up the hood, pushed on the right thing
and the car started as though it knew him.
Just doing his job. Didn't expect any thanks.
Doing what had to be done on a cold winter afternoon.

But Something laughed in me and clapped my hands
as though he just had danced.
He grinned, surprised and pleased,
and bowed.

evelyn flint

Her house is on the hill,
with a clear view across the mountains
and with all the sky.
Things are in order here,
and birds sing in the trees.
She keeps her house, her lawn, her garden
the way she keeps her life.

She's raised three children here,
and raised them right,
and now she coveys grandchildren
with whole-hearted laughter —
and berry pies.
"She's everything," they say,
and that she almost seems to be —
faithful daughter, attentive wife, loyal friend,
and what she is, she is
like rivers and like trees.

She remembers things we strain our eyes to see,
another time we never knew
and yet are homesick for —
days of logging and sawmills and maple syrup,
of trudging through snow to the one-room schoolhouse,
a family of thirteen children —
a time when life was harder day to day,
but clearer, too.

Her church stands on the other hill,
clean and tall,
with windows opening onto trees and sky,
and white walls remembering.
It seems that Sunday couldn't come without her here,
but then it never has to.
She teaches Sunday school, the adult class,
teaches that there is one God,
that His way is straight,
and that His arm is strong.
And she plays the organ
that lights these walls like candles,
opens windows in our hearts,
sets this hour on a hill.

For those of us whose houses are in valleys,
whose gardens fill with weeds,
whose faith is like the sun on cloudy days,
Evelyn, sure of her God as we are sure of her,
is like that one constellation you can always find,
no matter where you are.
And when you take your bearings
on the Big Dipper,
it gives you the North Star.

czelslavia (celia) bryke bailey

Imagine a topsy-turvy church
and everything all askew
with muddy footprints down the isle
and smudges on the pew.

Imagine a helter-skelter place
with cobwebs in each crack,
a communion table never laid —
everything out of whack.

Could Mary sit at Jesus' feet
and listen with whole heart,
without her sister Martha's care
could she have the better part?

Could we as well enjoy the warmth
of fellowship and prayer
within this ordered, peaceful house,
without Ciel Bailey's care?

The oldest of eight children,
a supervisor, too,
you have had a lot of practice
telling people what to do.

You have had a lot of practice, too
In courage and in daring,
In hard work and in faithfulness,
In loving and in caring.

You have taught our children Sunday School,
and taught them right and tough —
Even the Japanese you taught,
to turn a proper cuff.

You shake your finger at us,
and you have been known to frown,
but you're there when we need you,
and you never let us down.

And there's a sparkle in your eye,
a lively sense of fun —
when we're worth our salt, when the joke is good,
it comes out like the sun.

We're glad you tell it like it is,
and keep us all on track;
we're glad we pulled our socks up
and straightened up our act,

for those who care enough to keep
a house and heart like you,
are few and far between these days —

They don't make 'em like they used to.

the zen of plumbing

I have a lot to finish up.
Just found out I may not live to 100.
Need to finish my novel, organize my house,
pay my bills, write my obituary,
see if I can finally get that poem right.

A lot to finish up, and now
I have to stop to deal with this
bathtub that won't drain.
You've come over to help, so
I have to stop, no way around it,
go down cellar with you and hold the light,
look in the cabinet for that fitting you need —
a nut, you call it.
No way out of this one,
no way I could just sit here
trying to get that poem right.

You let me help, show me
 how this pipe goes in there, show me
all the stuff built up inside it, explain to me
what "we" are trying to do, tell me
where you need the light, ask me for things.

Finding the right nut is like getting an A+.
I remember now. I have done this before in other lives.
I can do this.
I would turn myself upside down
to get that light in the right spot.

I watch you, standing there
with two pieces of pipe, one in each hand,
putting together the answer as though they were all there is,
all there ever was,
as though the salvation of the world depends on it.

And then I get it!
It does.

Places

mont sainte victoire

Without foothill erupts the mountain, loud
booming genie, at its magic name:
these thunderstorms without a warning cloud,
this sea's blue, this sun's heat, these smiles burst the same
as from this land of limited palette, this source
of gray.
          Nor earth, nor growth, sienna-green,
smooths evident angularity or force
of planes, nor time nor storms the clear ravine.

Was it from Sainte Victoire you learned your way
of seeing other mountains, and every sight?
Or did you dream it first, and then one day
choose to paint it, finding it so right?

Views that become the visions of my mind
some inward landscape causes me to find.

market of provence (rondeau)

Market of Provence in sculpturing sun
and in crescendoing sound so sudden grown
from evening's empty square, and sudden gone.
Slow and cool the gesturing begun
all this gay commerce brightens in the sun
in color and in ripeness and in tone.
Market of Provence
and field, merchant and farmer here are one:
this day he shows and smiles, but he has sown
watered and watched and lost and reaped alone.

Nor loneliness nor love is ever done.

saint véran

You would have wondered why the winding road
climbed on so far beyond the last chalet
had you not known of Saint Véran; and you
still wonder that its there, at all. The way
you'd find a garden in a wilderness.
But it's no garden. Dark plain logs,
none but that is needed where it is,
and going all to make the houses all
face south, a storm-turned herd, unanimous weathervane.

The cold is unbelievable. You come
from where the autumn gold endures — almost
enough, and half of winter is the hope
of spring; and then you come at night.
                                              It's not
till morning, when the sun begins its stage
between two southern mountains, that you know
of Saint Véran, how it is there at all,
and why it faces south.

                   Push of storm
and pull of sun has swung around Saint Véran
the way it had to go — and held it there.

While no soft Indian summer insidiously
has whispered, «Why?»

                        Fortunate high hermit,
cold and night enough force your corporate prayer.

cannes

Cannes
by your long beaches and your soft brown sands
and by the loosely-fastened, languorous fans
of your palm trees, and by your waves
caressing shore in counterpoint —

Cannes
by your lush roses and your lemon trees,
your overflowing cup, your casual ease
stretched out beneath striped parasols —
by all your cultivated paradise

longing for the leeward side is filled,
born of the steepness and the wind unstilled
for weeks, and summer never soon
enough for years: complete port
                            Cannes.

Cannes
who has not come to you at his strength's end,
yet knowing too that he must turn again,
has not known harbor. Haven is here,
thank God! But heaven is further on.

proof

Two weeks ago I dreamed
a southern beach —
soft sand warm wind blue sea, the
whole sky and all the stars,
presided by a new constellation
brighter than Orion —
Leo, set with Jupiter and Mars.

Since then I've lived
a northern April
staying in out
of the rain
cleaning the house
doing my in-
come tax
(watching spring come out of the corner of my eye)

until tonight the rain stopped,
and I opened the door and
went out —
There, where the clouds were clearing,
after all

was an old constellation
brighter than Orion —
Leo, set with Jupiter and Mars.

welch mountain

The book says there is a mountain there,
but where we leave the car we cannot see it.
" ... woods road ½ mi ... abandoned hut
trail to NW ... marked by cairns ..."
Gradual and broad, the road runs before the wind
to the 'hut' — a chimney and a hearth
(Someone lived there once and could again.)
Then NW trail beats windward,
single and steep.
Up is hard
and sweet.
One and sure against our sure pace,
it brings us to an old place
in ourselves, on a new mountain.

Up first through woods, then onto open ledge
changing the landscape by each step,
and when we think we're at the top,
we see the top
up higher.

Up what was whole and dome
and now is planes of stone,
first one
and then the next.
Up the immediate mountain.

We sense the summit . . . what is it?
A hint (as sand is, of the sea).
At some point
trees dwarfing and boulders gianting
the mountain of the mountain
has swelled out of our climbing.

view behind
ahead climb
ledge ahead
ledge behind
steep ahead
steep behind
view behind
ahead climb

view ahead
the world spread
burst and settled from the swollen mountain.

Come once; and may not come again
by so clear path to so clear place.

the salt marsh

Cordgrass comes first,
broad-leaved and tough,
wherever shifting sands have made a cove,
sending new stems out of its sturdy roots,
making itself an island —
yet swaying on the surface with the waves.
It needs the tidal waters twice a day,
and twice a day they come.

Slowed by the grass, the sea
lets go its sediment that, with the grass,
dying in the fall,
becomes the higher soil
of next spring's higher grass.

Salt meadow grass comes next like silken hair,
taking the place of marsh grass
as the islands grow.
It needs the spring tide waters twice a month,
and twice a month they come.

Then come glasswort and lavender near the pools,
blackgrass and spikegrass along the edges,
algae among the tangled blades.
Snails and crickets eat the grass,
clams and mussels sift the tides,
crabs sift the mud,
feeding the grass and fish with phosphorous.

Sparrows and black ducks eat the snails
beside the Great Blue Heron,
while long-billed whimbrels burrow after crabs.
Crickets and ants and bugs that feast on grass
are feasted on by dragonflies and beetles,
and these are feasted on by birds.
Marshgrass feeds the fish
that, dying, are born
back to feed the grass.

Nothing is good or evil,
and nothing lasts, or ends.
All shelter all, and each by all is fed —
tides and the grass, the living and the dead.

you can't get here from there

Having gone there
by the long way
to walk, giants, in a wood
that every trunk and twig of
was traced by snow
sifted by fine sunlight
to collapse in crystal tinkling . . .

Having come there
by the lost way
where the trailed scarf of wind
whipped a sudden ghost up
to collapse in crystal tinkling . . .

Having come to timberline
I came to there in me
where eyes feel, feet understand and fingers see,
and came to there in you.

From the mountain
from me
from you
we have
descended
from there to here
to where we'd come from.

But it was damp and fresh and new,
just settling in again,
as though —
Was it gone too
while we were gone?

Then we have been far.

alaska

There is the den of winter
where the white wolf keeps his way
across the trackless tundra.
There is the lair of silence
where gaunt dark prayers of spruce
wait for stillness and snow.
There is the home of wilderness
my acre of stone-fenced woods remembers.

Seas of Beethovian mountains
like ancient oceans echo into night,
Denali dawns like Jehovah,
and hymns of dazzling shadows haunt the crystal sky.

There sun and moon and stars,
and maybe gods are fickle,
but in the crevices of winter,
the hearth of human love
shines like an alpine flower.

Sure silent wolf,
trophy of my binoculars,
O thou, at home in this vast glorious indifference,
walk there for me
in that cold royal hinterland of my soul.

voyage to the end of the world

I have set the flag of my heart
between the Andes and the Sea
on the long land of Chile —
dark eyes, clear smiles, a rhythm in the walk,
and talk like fountains — life
lived close to the skin, juicy
as sweet ripe peaches,
against the long time of mountains,
the still work of wine, aging in cool cellars
beneath the hastening vineyards.

In the streets of Santiago, I have found
the Paris of my youth, a certain spring
in Florence, a Spain I had imagined,
and, one night that lasts forever,
their music found my secret Latin loins
and taught me its hot dance.
Chile, hybrid of Old World mind and New World heart,
of conquistador and pioneer and Jesuit,
of Indian and immigrant, harvest and silver,
ferment and silence.

There is a whole continent down here,
quite complete, thank you, with its own history,
its own 'doesn't everyone?' way of looking at things
— even its own stars,
where January means long sun-filled days,
and sailing south means sailing into cold.
Back in fifth grade, they must have taught me that.
Now I learn it.

You board your ship at Puerto Monti,
then sail for days
a timeless maze of inland passage
through ancient presence of rough rounded hills,
fierce distance of snow streaked Andes,
great frozen rivers of tidewater glaciers —
world of the Creation
that never heard of man,
beginningless and endless
and enough.

Another day, and you have sailed northeast
into the Straits of Magellan.
Punta Arenas, then, a palette of bright roofs
to light the heart in this most southern port,
the way those sudden turquoise and purple and pink
houses of Quebec light northern winters.
Punta Arenas, far outpost, harbour
to all the nations of the world.

Now, doubling back, you continue down the coast,
still in that timeless maze of inland passage,
to the Beagle Channel, still further south.
Halfway through, you pass a little town,
humbly lichened on steeps of rock
between the tempering sea and sheltering crags.
A tender brings aboard the Argentine pilot.
Then Ushuaia, the town at the end of the world.
But these fields of daisies and clover,
these roadside dandelions tell you
you have not traveled as far as you think.

Cont. ⟶

voyage to the end of the world cont.

Tomorrow we will round the Horn, the cape
of huge triangular swells and treacherous winds
that drowned the ancient mariners in sailing ships.
We awake at dawn, our ship laboring against
heavy gray seas, and there it lies,
surfaced dripping in the mist,
like some great crusty monster of the deep.
Barnacles of buildings, just a couple,
crouch in a hollow on its back —
an outpost of the Chilean navy,
emblem of mankind.
On the hill, like two giant figures in silhouette,
the wings of the statue of the albatross,
soul of those unknown shipwrecked sailors
who in this hour become our kin.

And here they are, come out to welcome us,
those great wild creatures of the wind,
whose giant wings lean surely on the gales
that toss men's ships.
They follow us now as we run east, cantering on the waves.
One whole day they glide and soar,
white breasts shining like joy as they sweep high,
dark wings coasting like faith as they sweep low,
and, in the evening, at our stern,
garlanding a huge pink sun
that sets into the sea.

In the morning, we lay off Port Stanley,
the Falkland Islands we had never heard of
until that strange sudden war
from nowhere, and from a hundred years of history.
Going ashore, we walk the quiet streets
of English gardens and English pubs.
We rest awhile in the little Anglican cathedral,
marriage of Westminster and this proud, humble land.
In the afternoon, we cross the Scottish moors
and Cornish beaches to find South American
black penguins on white sands.

Three days at sea now, going north
back to the summer's warmth of January.
Time to stand by the rail and join the breathing
of that same sea we dreamed on when we were twenty,
time to lie back into the waves
and take a nap, time to read that book.

Morning in Montevideo, city of beaches and parks,
of oleander and hibiscus and trees from many climates,
city of soft air and openness and light,
stable, prosperous, a little dull —
Switzerland between two hostile giants.
I miss the quick smiles of Chile.
At evening we sail out
past the hill with the fort on top,
into the shallow waters of the bay where
we are piloted all night toward Buenos Aires.

voyage to the end of the world cont.

The Paris of South America, they call it.
Yes, the fashion and the pulse,
the street performers — here it's the tango,
that dueling dance in torrid red, flared nostrils,
grease-slicked hair, dark passion.
Yes, the Sunday strolls of families and lovers,
the restaurants with white tablecloths.
Yes, but something missing —
those 17th century buildings,
those old stone churches
that sang to me of Paris in Santiago.

Our last day. We head for the estancia
across the pampas, too close to urban sprawl
to have that vastness we have read of —
flat, but not the sea-like flatness of our plains.
An island kind of day to dwell in warmth
and dappled shade, to watch horseback exploits
of mustachioed gauchos with black sombreros,
of boy gauchos with dreams of cattle herding,
to get up on a horse again after all these years
and feel the solid soft of sheepskin blanket,
to share a bitter, refreshing sip of maté
and eat barbecued beef we can never forget.
Tourists, not cattle, are the real business here,
but still we glimpse that brief heroic past,
moment of rustlers and herders and empty pampas.

Tomorrow we fly home.
I have grown by a hemisphere.

the outgroup

Moths
were always useless bugs
to be screened out,
to fly at light bulbs
and be swept up,
pests to be mothballed and moth proofed against,
not grace, design and poetry
like gold and azure waltz of butterflies.

Then yesterday,
in this strange desert of New Mexico,
I heard the story of the rare evening primrose,
treasure of these rough mountains
where cactus bloom by day,
it opens only at night,
and is pollinated by
moths.

And today,
as I came home along the canyon trail,
in cool of sunset shadow
and freshening birdsong,
the soft yellow of the evening primrose
opened for me.

Grace, design and poetry
by those moon-colored artists of the night!

my polish freighter

Somewhere

on Lake Erie, maybe,
maybe sailing like smooth swans on the St. Lawrence
through a sunset evening in Québec,
Somewhere
bearing back across the North Atlantic, maybe,
maybe cantering on those prehistoric swells
from distant ancient storms
that rear and buck bright manes of fireworks
across the forecastle.
Or maybe on her course across the cold North Sea,
rolled by white-capped leviathans
in a near-gale gray
that hurls the dishes back and forth across the table
and slops your guts like water.
Somewhere
her high shape that is man's answer to the sea,
Somewhere the Iryda sails.

Somewhere
her cheery steward hurries,
doing everythingatonceeverywhere, but always
with a love, yes, a real love of doing well,
Somewhere
in a sheltered spot on deck, her Chief Mecanik
takes an hour in the sun, or, docked in port,
rides his bike off to explore,
while the oldest officer works on a slide show
to send his grandson.
Somewhere those Able Seamen with the hardy smiles
hose down the decks or paint the hatches,
take turns at the helm
when the pilot is on board, repair the ship's cranes,

or, maybe, in a sweet evening
somewhere
drift silent out on deck to watch the sunset.
Somewhere the Iryda sails.

These Polish sailors do their jobs
shipshape and right,
and that includes the cook.
Trained professionals, they love good Polish sausage
and funny videos.
On a Sunday morning, after being up early to get docked,
they sit a long time around the breakfast table,
laughing and talking.
Sailing past Hamlet's castle or in the Norwegian fiords,
they are out with cameras and binoculars,
as delighted as any tourist, probably more,
and they have T-shirts from Ecuador and Houston,
from Panama and Milwaukee.
But their cell phones, the best you can buy,
give them away.

Everywhere
a descant with a lyric melody
vines
through the shipshape and the videos,
the cameras and the T-shirts.
A song of absence
a song of Poland
a song of a beautiful wife
and children with sweet smiles
a dog with big brown eyes
a kerchiefed grandmother
on her ninetieth birthday
with all the sisters and the cousins
around a table in the garden.

Cont. ⟶

my polish freighter cont.

Somewhere
her Kapitan is pacing
on the Bridge, like a football coach on the sidelines,
living the crew, the ship, the wind,
sole master under God.
Somewhere
her Chief Mate, in jumpsuit and helmet, does his steep job
as gentle light as poet in disguise,
or, on his sunrise watch, keeps track of gauges,
keeps track of radar,
beholds the silent organ chords of dawn.
Somewhere
her Third Officer keeps his late night watch alone
on the darkened bridge
with the fog closed in, and the storm fraught prow.
One strong and fragile vessel of humanity
and the huge dark sea.
Somewhere the Iryda sails.

There sails my young adventurous soul,
keeping me tall and true and free.

flight from paris

I — LAST DAY IN PARIS

I want to walk along the quays again
in slanted summer of October light,
to take my favorite bridge across the Seine,
then buy hot chestnuts coming home tonight.

I want to call to say my last goodbyes,
to picnic in the Luxembourg at noon,
and buy that pillow for you — a surprise
that lights my mind like a huge orange moon.

A cornucopia of dreams, a cup
of time. Some will slip through like silver fish.
A traffic light, a bus just pulling up,
an opening in the crowd, a subway missed,
are only roulette numbers, even or odd —
The openings in my heart are acts of God.

II — CLOSING THE DOOR

I've swept your house more sweetly than my own,
I've made your bed, I've made it smooth and tight,
and placed, to catch your eye on coming home,
the new pillow by your window in the light.

I will be already gone a long time then
to where my hands can't help you any more,
or move the pillow's place one inch. But when
you come at last, I'll just have closed the door.

Now, at the window, take the opiate
of golden crowns of trees in waltzing flow,
and glimpse, across the centuries of slate,
my own young autumns here a life ago.

Time to leave now. The airplane will not hold
for all my careful hands or miser's gold.

III — THE AIRPORT

My bags are checked, my seat has been assigned.
We raw recruits of heaven, duty-free,
haunt stand-up bars or vaguely wait in line,
becalmed by limbo's swift lobotomy.

Some things I've done, some I had to leave.
My money has been spent or given away —
I will not need it now. How easily
I let go all I held to yesterday!

My flight is called, my turn has come around
to set forth up that westward corridor
and find at last the mystery they found,
those gay deserting backs that went before.

Now we lift off, pull up our wheels and, light,
move in another way, beyond your sight.

IV — THE FLIGHT

We lift from earth like kites of sleep,
forget the tangle of our moorings there,
let fall the city like a cloak, and leap
into the other hammocks of the air.

Now Paris, like a lifetime, maps its trees
and boulevards in years. The Sacré Coeur,
the Eiffel Tower emerge like memories
of songs and streets and sunrises that were.

Convoyed by fleets of clouds, our shadow form
among the shadows of the clouds in driven,
then, drowning through the temple of the storm,
the roof of earth becomes the floor of heaven!

We sojourn in eternity. Then, too soon,
the New World rises like a dawning moon.

It's About This Flower

it's about this flower

You say
that we are going to do ourselves in
but,
looked at from the stars,
the universe will survive.
I say
we are tired travelers
tempted to sleep in the snow
and the part that belongs to God
can let go
but the part that belongs to earth
has to hold on
has to try to find a way
because
we can see the universe in one flower
but they can't see this flower from the stars.

the pilgrims

Leaving England
they had to breathe leaving
into skin and blood,
had to let leaving
fill them like a flood,
like a lover.

They had to sail an Ocean without continents,
had to become an alien race
living on struggle and storm,
except for truce of evening
or amnesty of morning,
except for a bird's flight,
for the touch of a hand,

And only then America.

as though
the real pilgrimage
is not to America,
but to struggle and storm,
to a bird's flight,
to the touch of a hand.

out out damn spot

Better than blood of lamb
sacrificed
or Isaac son of Abraham
or even Christ
Son of Man

or suicide or accident,
at last the full equivalent
of nameless crime —
disaster equal to our sense of doom!

LIFE HALF-MAST BY DALLAS
TOTAL ECLIPSE BY MEMPHIS

ANCIENT MINOTAUR
HAPPENS HORROR IN ASIAN WAR

PROMETHEUS WON OUT
SUN'S SECRET PUTS SUN OUT

Fire of hell, or heaven.

Or else these human
hands dirty hands
that can be washed for supper
in soap and water
better than blood of any son of man.

written at the time of the Vietnam War.

let's boycott the war and go to the olympics

We are too much afraid
of fear of death,
and not enough afraid
of death.

We cover their coffins
with the flag,
their groans
with the national anthem,
and their graves
with flowers —

but only during the commercials.

We keep busy
buying and selling gold,
going on diets,
and waiting for God
to come down the chimney.

We are too much afraid
of fear of death
and not enough afraid
of death,

so we play war
as though it were a game,
instead of games
as though they were a war.

written while the US was deciding whether to boycott the 1980 Moscow Summer Olympics.

tug of war

London Bridge is falling
down
fall —
ling
down.
The Montagues and the Capulets
are at it again,
and the Quaker boy demonstrating for peace
can't stand the lady at the desk,
can't see she's just trying so hard
to do the right thing
that sometimes she goes too far,
and the Tory woman
who was an air-raid warden in WWII
calls them "them",
and no one knows that
what things seem to be
is part of what they are.

London Bridge is falling down,
my fair lady!
Which flavor do you want?
Chocolate or vanilla,
Liberal or Conservative,
Argentine or British?

Missionary to the heathen
Or prophet in his own land?

written at the time of the Falklands War.

the florida recount

The Greek Tragedies of our time
are played on the Stage of TV screens, echoing
around the world like the fireworks of Y2K.
The Theater is our bars and fitness clubs, our living rooms,
our minds —
the riderless horse for JFK,
the flowers for Princess Di,
Vietnam, Kuwait, Sarajevo, Kosovo,
Election Year 2000.

Our hearts resound with unexpected heroes —
a lawyer, ready as an athlete,
lightfooted champion against a lumbering fate,
four judges, grandparents in black robes,
sturdy enough to stand an ounce of chaos,
and people like us,
faithful and weary,
counting ballots by hand around a table
on the frontline of democracy.

The counting stopped.
The country stopped. By order of the court.
We know too little about the truth now,
and we know too much.
Something less than the wisdom of Solomon
has chosen the flaws of machines over the flaws of man.
In mid-act
the curtain falls.

One actor is left to take his bows,
his inauguration balls, his Air Force One, his roses.
The other has slipped out the stage door,
taking his wife by the hand.

One morning, after a sleepless night,
he will go for a walk alone at dawn,
a wild fox will run across his path,
sandpipers will skitter under the waves,
and a red sun will be born out of the sea.

tsunami 2005

In the New Year, they said,
there will be cell phones
you can watch TV on,
and more humane forms of torture.
You will be able to buy a car
that drives itself,
and legs and arms and ears and heads
will be cut off.

They said there will be a pill to cure obesity,
and canaries will drop dead in the street.
They didn't say the stage itself
of all our puny dreams
could crack, could crash, could crumble,
could shift on its axis, labor and deliver
a barreling mountain of water
to sweep it all away —
the terrorists, the polluters, the honeymooners,
the rich tourists, the poor fishermen,
and that we wouldn't be able to blame it
on any one, not even on God,

and that only the fierce and gentle things,
like the will to love each other's faults,
cannot be swept away,
for only these will have lived.

another kind of flag

How can I —
walking my baby at 3 a.m.,
cutting my wood against the north country winter,
doing my homework, listening to my friend,
limping with my cane,
how can I stand with them
who ran up the stairs to save those running down,
who search in smoke and rubble on 12 hour shifts,
who light a candle for one
who does not come and does not come and does not come —
how can I stand with them?

Walk my baby with their heart,
cut my wood with their care,
let my homework be a hymn,
let my listening be a candle,
march with my cane.

Live this day, this hour
as though they were watching me —
taste this maple turning red beside my door,
smell these damp leaves, hear the silence, feel the sun,
see that grand waltz of treetops in the wind,
be the clear answer of a single violin.
Hold on
let go
try again.

the way out

Pure bluegold September morning.
We are sitting at our desks, going to the water cooler,
sorting the mail, talking on the phone,
knowing an hour is sixty minutes, a table is a table,
some people are better than others,
the world is round and we will live forever.

Sudden black boom smash shatter black
end of the world.
Silence, smoke, me alone.

Then, out of the darkness, a flashlight and a voice,
"Here, take my hand. I know the way out."

I grab hold of the man with the light who knows the way,
and, with my other hand, I reach out
to the friend beside me and
he finds the hand of the boy with the blue hair and
he the neighbor with the noisy machine and
he the relative who thinks she's always right and
she the one who can never get her act together and
the smartass and the loser and the couch potato and
the nerd and the creep and the snob and
the jock and the jerk and the slob and
the procrastinator and the perfectionist and
the one with the messy desk,

all followers, all leaders, behind this other Noah.

revelations

This time he did not come in a cloud
he did not come in a burning bush
or in a pillar of fire
he did not speak in thunder from the mountain.
This time he did not walk on the sea
or turn stones into bread
he did not raise the dead.
This time he was not born in Bethlehem.

I saw him born like a revolution of gold
forsythia, on a thousand winter bushes
I saw him spread like a beautiful epidemic
I heard him come like water in the woods
seeping, then trickling
then springing streaming flowing
from a thousand mountains through a thousand forests
down a hundred rivers to the Sea.

I saw two rival powers rendezvous in space,
plant the whole earth's flag on the moon
and learn each other's language.
I saw the arsenals all closed
the soldiers all come home
and the world feeding the world.
This time he did not come in a cloud
he did not walk on the sea
he was not born in Bethlehem.
He was born like gold forsythia
and he came like water in the woods
when one then two then three
then cities and then nations
then you and I were free
to dare to hold our hands out
down the rivers to the Sea.

stars, asters
and other lighthouses

What we have here
are these tectonic plates and
these tropical depressions and
these cryospheres.
But what about
these tiny lavender flowers at land's end,
these lovers with naked bodies,
these friends with naked hearts,
this Beethoven's Ninth Symphony.

Maybe
those deep rivers at the bottom of our souls
flow
from the same well
as hurricanes and earthquakes.
And maybe not.

But if they do,
and we could get that frequency coming in clear
through the cranky static of bullheadedness,
and we could tune our ear to that deep song,
deeper, I think even than despair,

then maybe we could know
when to head for shore and
when to seek higher ground,
where to build our houses,
and that it is O.K. to die.

And if we know,
then we could be lighthouses
there
every night
like stars
whether or not
there happens to be
a ship lost at sea.

Cranberry Lake

the cardinal flowers

Yes, yes! they are just right,
there where they have opened overnight —
just what we meant to say
and couldn't find the words!
With all this brown and gray
and all this blue and green of woods and lake,
a flash of scarlet shows.
Oh, it's not needed, heaven knows,
but it is genius.

It's not by chance they grow
here where he transplanted years ago
the wild ones. She asked him to.
She'd seen them growing by the brook, and knew
they could grow here.

She's dead
who first loved them for being red,
and he's alive, but gone away.
They go ahead,
though, now it's up to them.
Look how they've spread,
even. That's the thing! It's more
than that they just survive
the same — it's that some even thrive
apart, here and there along the shore.

sleight of cloud

You know one of those days
of high-flying clouds,
trailing dark greens
across the light green hill,
when — if you don't look up and only look out,
you'll see clear shadow and clear sunshine will
each possess the fields fully,
and pass.
Each seems lasting,
but neither seems to last.

Yes, I know, we know well the way
something as soft and slow
as a white cloud
drifting
can change the Yea to Nay.

cathedral window

Along the end of summer trail
the woods were green and brown,
and, not to fall or lose my way,
my eyes were looking down.

Around a bending of the trail
a red leaf lies
I see it in my breast
as I feel it with my eyes.

The sun shines on it
and it shines on me,
the brightest thing that I can see.
Then I look up
and behold the Tree!
The sun shines through it
straight to me.

Along the end of summer trail
my eyes were looking down
so not to fall or lose my way —
but that red leaf
that the sun lights
has come
so not to lose my other way
by a tree that lights the sun.

indian summer

For you there, on our island,
counting days by notches on a stick,
not counting hours at all,
this truce
of Indian summer
must come as a gift,
as a cove behind the wind.

Last night what warmth you had
came from your fire, your bed,
your thoughts.
No weatherman to herald
this velvet-petaled dawn,
opening like orchids.

For you there, in the silence
of our forgotten mother-tongue,
riding the waves of where
you are,
knowing the pathway of the sun,
this crystal room
must come
as another chance at Eden.

inspiration

I saw something beautiful
last night while you were gone —
beside the silver waterfall,
a golden doe and fawn!

Yes! I know just where it was —
I always used to think
that everything waited there at dusk
for a deer to come and drink.

Come, let's go together now —
it's that same time of night,
and that same kind of weather now,
and the wind is right!

This is the magic place
for the golden doe and fawn!
This is the hour of grace . . .

. . . but the deer do not come.

visitor

Here in my lean-to at the end of the island,
I surprise a waning orange moon,
forgotten grail,
rising late and later.

I come out on that sweet remembered sky,
still there, after all this time,
those same near stars
of that summer here alone,

I see Jupiter,
descended to our hills,
touch the water with its pathway
like a moon.

And, in the morning,
two clear cedar waxwings
tick about their life,
and do not know I watch.

Here where this lives,
I may approach,
camouflaged in stillness,
bearing the white flag of my solitude.

When will it come to me
in that hubbub
of wanting and fearing
where I live?

days

Here, with the lake opening the sky,
I can never say, "Tomorrow
I will do this," because tomorrow
the wind will blow from its own direction.

One day a lemon-apricot dawn focuses
into a lazy, dawdling sun; the next,
a northeast gale rolls swells from
distant continents across my bay.
I say goodnight to orchestras of stars
and awake to soft, releasing rain.

Yesterday, blessed by the evening sun,
the woods came on like lanterns;
this morning, primeval mist gives birth
to islands and to hills — temples,
whole in the glass lake
with their mysterious halves.

Each night leaves on the shores of day
my world in a new key —
gift, if I will take,
to the eyes of my blindness.

forever and a day

Tall light holy Height,
Hemlocks and Stars.
Still bright brilliant Night.
No move mars
Perfection.

Dark Chords glorious Chorus
Soundless resound.
Longed for ancient Forest,
Lost and Found:
Perfection.

Then resurrection ...
    Slowly the darkness and brightness
    has faded to gray
    and colors come
    and shining clouds are shot between the trees.

    Suddenly shimmering water
    has started to play
    and ripples run
    and glancing gold is dancing on the leaves ...

    Then a breeze
    swings the branches
    and they sway
    as they please
    with the breeze
    on a day that lasts a day ...

They that Stand with Stars together
On a Night that lasts Forever.

eternity has time

The view of the lake from the front porch
of the main house —
that was always one of our altars,
and always there was the old stump
in the foreground, a little to one side,
halfway between tree and earth.

It has made the landscape
of our sunsets and our thunderstorms,
our playing train in the swinging hammock,
our watching for a certain boat
to come up the lake,
the landscape of our looking up from a book
on a rainy afternoon, of solitary breakfasts,
of talk like wood fires,
the landscape of singing and guitar,
of our first kiss, our first broken heart.

And always there has been the old stump,
halfway between tree and earth.
But then one year, growing right straight
out of the top of it,
was a new seedling — a sure little spruce,
getting a head start in more ways than one.
Only then could I see
that the stump, lately, is more earth than tree.

Let's sit together on the front porch
sometimes, you and I,
in sunsets and in thunderstorms,
and watch how they are growing —
the stump toward earth,
sending the seedling from its center
toward the sky.

opening camp duet

We've spent a week here, you and I,
opening camp in June,
sweeping down the log walls,
wiping off tables and shelves with Murphy's,
washing the windows, pitching leftover junk,
putting down the rugs.

Let's take some time before we leave
to go around together,
take a good drink of all this open-ness we've made
preparing summer.

Now we can carry it home and keep it,
a cloth of beauty and order, woven
by our work
as we cleaned together in separate rooms,
trading brooms, buckets,
questions, little victories,

by our talk
as we sat at the table by candlelight,
walking barefoot
in the temple of each other's dreams,

by our dance
as we learned to move together
like that chamber orchestra
without a conductor.

summer home

"I guess I'm stuck with it,"
my son said once, affectionately,
of this old log house, where all of us,
for three generations,
have grown up summers,
where, now, we're starting to come home
to have our ashes scattered in the lake.

There's always something breaking or
falling apart or not working right —
a leak in a new spot, a window
that won't close, a door that sticks,
mice nests, bat droppings,
chipmunks getting into stuff, and

out in the middle of the lake,
on a clear night
you can see all the stars.

This year, a tree has fallen
on the lean-to roof,
the closet off the back porch
has got too much crammed into it again,
the dock is sinking on one side, and

one afternoon, my brother came and sat with me
in those old rocking chairs on the front porch,
and told me who he was.

red geraniums

August 2, 1998

We just don't get it
that you keep not showing up
coming down to the dock to welcome us,
curious about what we've become and done —
that we don't meet you gaily on the path
or find you doing crosswords in your chair.
Everywhere, it seems you were just there,
or are just about to come.

We almost hear that crisp warmth of your voice,
asking us things because you really want
to know, the way you did,
delighting us with talk of Italy or
grandchildren, or the book you'd just been reading,
telling Nelson not to be so pompous,
seasoning our lives with the pepper of your wit.
The way you were plays in us like a song.

We miss you when we've done something good
that wants to be admired,
or have a sore finger that needs sympathy.
We miss you worrying about us,
making us laugh,
pointing out things of beauty,
opening our minds.
There is an empty place at our table.

We find you in the tall shape of a red glass bottle,
in a certain careful shell, a vase of dried flowers,
an old bathtub painted blue.
We find you in the simplicity of these bare windows,
in an antique china teapot, a painting of Renaissance angels,
a pot of red geraniums.
These useless, necessary things glow
with your life still, and comfort us.

The sun sets, opening its colors to the sky.
So does your Irish charm and stubbornness bequeath to us
the grit to love fiercely,
the zest to adventure gaily,
the will to make a place for beauty,
the courage to be simple.
Our lives, more real, more passionate, can be
bright flowering bushes planted on your grave.

Like a book we loved and wished would never end,
we carry you in our hearts,
light as a feather
and powerful as the wind.

putting away summer

Finally, I get it,
after fifty years of closing camp,
I get it that we are acolytes,
that all these tasks of putting away Summer
are a ceremony
about this beautiful old house
whose resonant logs hold all our hours,
a ceremony about all of you, and them.

We have missed them here, everywhere,
in the clearing he made for us,
the buoy light at dusk
where we scattered their ashes,
her old canoe paddle,
we have found them here, everywhere.

And we have missed you here, everywhere,
in the new gutter you made,
the reopened path to my lean to
where you had cleared the fallen tree,
the poem left on my bed,
we have found you here, everywhere.

Here, maybe only here,
we can make a clear place,
the beds covered,
the canoes brought in,
the rugs and pillows packed away,
the floor swept.

When you open camp next summer,
you will find us here,
everywhere.

the buoy light

The windows of his house are all his eyes,
all summer long they've watched the lake with me.
The buoy light at dusk replies, replies.

We've watched the eighty summers of our lives
this place holds like an album. Can I see,
and the windows of his house be all his eyes?

When every path expects him to arrive,
can still each turn refuse him stubbornly?
The buoy light at dusk replies, replies.

What of the man, the songs that made him cry,
what of his laugh, what of his memories?
The windows of his house are all his eyes.

What of the boy, the boats he loved to drive,
what of his dreams? "Just this: remember me,"
the buoy light at dusk replies, replies.

But there was more to say before goodbyes —
O, shipmate, for another day at sea!
The windows of his house are all his eyes:
the buoy light at dusk replies, replies.

his canoe

You might think he was an old man, maybe,
watching him from a distance with his cane,
but his hair still grows in that same swirl
at the back of his neck
as when he was a little boy,
and he still yells at ball games.
He still plays to win
and loves what he loves
with the same terrier heart,
loves you, his grandson,
grown tall and straight and true,
loves the lake and man's answer to the lake,
the canoe.

Years ago, he bought this one, made to order for him
of pine — light and resonant,
nervous as a thoroughbred.
It has been his instrument, his passage
to the lake
to the beaver and the otter and the Great Blue Heron,
to the calm pools at the source of the lake,
to the ancient loon, his soul.

Now
his body won't go where his heart still goes,
so now
he has given you his canoe
and now
he can ride in your canoe
to the beaver and the otter and the Great Blue Heron,
to the calm pools, to the ancient loon,
and further
to rivers you had dreamed together,
and lakes beyond his dreams.

He will ride in your canoe
now, and always,
ready whenever you are,
with cheer to give you heart.

pilgrimage to the source

You have to go out from the house
and leave the dishes in the sink,
and the questions unanswered.
You have to put your canoe in the water
and push away from the shore.

Now you begin to paddle down the cove
between the islands
to the white birch trees
that seemed to be the end.

There you can round the point into the Flow.
Here is the home of the kingfisher
and the beaver and the Great Blue Heron,
and the wind from the lake is behind you now.

But still you have not gone far enough.
You have to paddle across the flow,
past the drowned trees, to the big rocks
that seemed to be the end.

Now you can pass through the channel into the Pool.
Here you can ship your paddle and drift
as the cardinal flowers on the beach come out,
one at a time, like stars at dusk.

Behind you, the waves still come in
from the lake, but here
the trees dream of themselves
in the calm water.

Then, from the other side,
like the moon at sunset,
comes the part you had forgotten —
the voice of the brook.

Belle Isle

leeward and windward

They live and love in their house
on the near side of the island.
It has windows to shut the wind
and lights to shut the night.
It has a bed
where they lie beside each other,
and her lips know his skin
and his hand knows her breast.
It has a table
where they sit across from each other,
and his eyes know her face
and her ears know his voice.
They give each other a name.

Sometimes he (or she) will go alone —
when he has had enough,
or not enough, of love —
to where the sea and rocks and he are one
on the far side of the island
where he grows as the heather grows
and blows as the weather blows
and ebbs and flows with the tide
(and where a tiny yellow flower
gives joy for the looking).
There he walks in sun and rain the same,
for the calling gulls never call his name.

In one he is found — here is his house ...
In the other he is lost — there is his home.

côte sauvage

Scarves of brown earth,
sheathed in tender pasture,
waltz
across the shoulders of stolid storms of rock,
massive adversaries of the open sea —
primeval fleet,
echoing down the coast like memory.

To the west,
a band of sliver darkness
outlines the darker sister of the sky.
To the south, a chord of silver light
dazzles
where the sea receives the beamed chorale
of the Lord on High.

From the deep-breathing swells
waves surface in sudden monsters,
threatening the land,
explode in celebrations on the stubborn rocks,
inhale in ladled waterfalls,
succumb in long caresses on the accepting sand.

Over the far cliff,
one single gull,
and beyond,
the Great Lighthouse.
Dune-grass and the dried stems of flowers
bend away from the wind.
Blind curtains of spray ghost in.

I move back from the edge and sit down,
placing both hands flat on the ground.
I have seen this all before, somewhere else,
ten thousand years ago
and yesterday.

port andro

You come from the other side.
Here, for the first time, you find
the south and noon
and your radiant water.
The rocks here, female
of those fist-clenched cliffs,
recline from the sea
in folds of harmony.
Sweet sonnet of presence,
held by those urgent fortresses against the deep.

You mount the path above the beach
to the balcony of your palace of rock,
and survey your queendom of the sea.
The canopy of sky hangs a soft cloth
of whispered colors
over your halls of air.
A fishing boat passes
to sound the vastness,
then a lone gull
to sound the solitude.

Port is the lost sister of the sea.

sauzon

Eight in the morning,
the old fisherman walks the port, waiting
for the young fishermen to come in.
Nine, the church tower lets go its hourly flight of chimes,
pulse of the quiet town.
Ten o'clock, and the basket-armed women
blow together and apart like autumn leaves
between the bakery and the general store.
Madame LePort has brought the cross of her parent's grave
down from the cemetery,
to clean and polish it for All Saint's Day.
Eleven, and the scavengers, men and gulls,
escort the tide out of the narrow bay.

Now Noon, and the stoop shouldered, cross eyed sexton,
pulling and pulling the heavy rope,
transcends himself into a festival of bells.
The old fisherman joins the young fishermen at the bar,
telling the new stories, the old stories;
stairways rejoice with the smells of garlic and laurel;
a lone woman roams the deserted flats,
gathering periwinkles in her pail.

One o'clock, bar and streets are empty.
The fishing boats, stranded by the tide,
lean on their crutches.
Two, and the town digests,
strolling the quay,
standing together in twos and threes,
watching the lazy ballet of the port.
Three, the son of the restaurateur has gone out again;
his mother has lost two sons at sea.

Four o'clock, and the sexton pulls the rope, now
slowly, as though to make a monument of sound.
The bell tolls, they have all known this man,
a young fisherman, an old fisherman, a scavenger in the bay.
The bell tolls, the priest leads up the road
to the cemetery above the town;
he holds the crucifix high, and the bell tolls;
the people on foot, in silence, follow the coffin,
follow the crucifix to the cemetery
where all their dead are buried,
where they will all be buried, and their children.

On the other side of the island
at the outpost of Land,
Leviathan rages against the Bastion Cliffs
in deadly combat.
But in Sauzon
he pastures pastel blue as the heart's Yea.
The town holds hands around the church,
its back toward the sea, its windows toward the sun.

island in the sea

There! There she is —
sculling his boat beside the quay,
no, there, climbing the rocks — no,
swimming far out there in the bay . . .
always just leaving when I come.
She has been living here for thirty years,
ever since I went away.
I wear the ring he gave her that last day,
but she still walks along the cliff with him,
and sails out in the sunrise with the waves
I look at from the shore.

There! There he is —
there in that old look of your eyes,
no, there, laughing at me — no,
there in the way you stopped short in surprise . . .
flickering like shadows in the wind.
He has been in my heart for thirty years,
as a star is in the sky.
We talk about the old times, you and I,
but they still walk around the port together,
and taste the air and touch the long July
of pictures in my drawer.

There! There they are —
there through the clouds, that virgin blue,
no, there, walking home late — no,
talking the way they used to do . . .
blown by like a scent of secret flowers.
They have been in bloom for thirty years,
since I said goodbye to you.
Oh, something weeps in me for horse drawn plows,
for wooden shoes and cobblestones and lace,
a boat with yellow sails, a certain house . . .
Where, where are they?

The hold clangs shut. The faces on the quay,
the port, the cliffs pulled into yesterday.
A long haired girl, beside me at the rail,
stands watching backward, watching all the way . . .
There, there she is.

wanderfreund

That's what the label says.
It must be made in Germany, or maybe Austria,
for hikers in the Alps, with backpacks and shorts
and cleated boots, striding with sure, muscled legs.
Not for an old woman,
out of breath, off balance,
everything askew, propped up or artificial —
her own teeth, though.

Not for an old woman,
coming back to an island
where her young self still bikes and walks all day,
swims for hours off empty beaches
or into little bays you can't get to any other way,
sails out at daybreak with the mackerel fleet.

Not for an old woman
coming back to an island
where her young self calls to her from every path.
Not for an old woman,
wanting to answer that call.
But a mile is longer now, a hill steeper.

And then here, here it is,
a walking stick
that can be adjusted to just the right length,
that is light, but strong,
has an ergonomic soft cork handle,
and, best of all, a rubber tip for roads
that pulls off to reveal a spike for dirt paths!

Yes, here it is!
Not an old woman's cane,
but a wanderfreund.
Here it is,
my hero's staff, my sorcerer's broom, my sword of fire.

Here it is.
And here I am.
Yes, I am coming!

Night Work

night work

Sleep drugs the doorman of my day,
the demons and the spirits of my night
spill out to play
their dances of demention and delight.

My sly third eye has watched at dawn,
and caught them at their dancing on my green.
Then they were gone,
and all I see denies what I have seen.

All except love and death. Those gifts
of night release the day to love and die,
to die and live,
to swim with rivers and breathe in the sky.

perennials

This year, tired of weeding,
we laid a patio
of smooth brick tiles,
but soft as warm asphalt, maybe because
something somewhere in us
remembered
we had made a garden there last year.

And now — beautiful big artichokes
grow, have grown
bubbling under the asphalt
bursting through perfect
round ripe full
like giant green cones,
and there are plenty of them,
plenty.

And we can pick them,
cup them round, lift them with both hands
like a ripe chalice . . .

and inside,
when we have peeled and eaten
a thousand luscious leaves,
will be the heart.

the heroine

She is the daughter of God
and the sister of the wind.
Straight and supple as grass,
she stands brown on the long white sand,
robed in nakedness.
The waves are her breath,
the gulls her heart,
the sea her inheritance.
She is our history and our dream,
the priestess and the lamb.

Now she begins her walk into the water
like a bride,
like a criminal to execution;
and the sea becomes a cool cathedral,
embracing her like clouds.
She breathes with gills now.

Then she is born out of the sea,
a goddess
with necklaces of water and a seaweed crown,
born on that far beach from which she drowned.

shadow liberation

Somehow my shadow has come to life!

Sometimes she follows me as shadows should
and at some noons
she is me.

But sometimes she stays behind or goes ahead
or thinks the opposite of what I say
or plays with me as though I were a doll
or watches me as though I were a play.

And when I sleep she dreams.

I always thought, and so did she
that a stranger was a stranger
and that even you were only you.
But suddenly I knew
that the one in me that watches me
is your shadow too.

moonlighting

If you've ever caught the moon
disguised as a cloud
just happening by
in the afternoon . . .

and then if you have thought
that innocent passer-by
still moves the tides . . .

then you'll know the way it was
when I caught, behind the scenes,
the director of my strangers and my friends
and all my selves,
and knew her for
the dreamer of my dreams.

my apartment in paris

I

I have this apartment in Paris
I never seem to get a chance to use.
The address is at home somewhere,
but I can't remember where I put it.
I've kept forgetting to send the rent —
I even keep forgetting I have the apartment.

But, now that I'm in Paris, I remember,
and worry that they won't have held it for me.
So I hurry to go and pay the rent.
The landlady is all the crazy ladies I have known,
and lives with lots of gypsies
in a shadowy cellar.

They still have the apartment for me,
but the rent is three months overdue.
I reach for my wallet, amazed these gypsies
have not stolen it, and start to pay.
Then the landlady explains that,
due to inflation and death,
they have to raise the rent.

I pay, and leave, kissing the gypsies all goodbye.
On my way, I stop to take a calling card
beside the door. It turns out
my landlady is a crazy gypsy poet
who lives in New York,
and says she is my fairy godmother.

II

I am homesick for my apartment in Paris,
and look all over for it —
in Paris and New York,
next door, and in the next room.
I know I've seen it somewhere before.

Then I remember where . . . It was
walking alone along the beach,
or looking out my window at the trees,
or listening to silence . . .

My apartment in Paris
is the wave-length of my soul!

the far room

The motel is on a lagoon,
so the sign says.
When I go in, it turns out
the 'lagoon' is a swimming pool,
rectangular and concrete,
with so many measured cubic feet
of swimming-pool-blue water.
The motel units are docked along each side
like little houseboats,
fully equipped and
perfectly white and square.
All around are other motels
on other lagoons.

"But a lagoon has always been
a swimming pool, Madame,"
says the lady at the desk,
"I don't care what you thought."
She shows me to my room
out near the end.
"You get two for the price," she says,
"at this motel. Which one do you want
for your other room —
the one across the hall,
or the one adjoining,
further out on the same side?"
I choose the far one.

When I go in, I see
it is out at the very end, and
its window opens onto
change and flow and endlessness,
colors remembering,
stillness that breathes, that flickers . . .
A soft depth receives my eyes
and bathes my face — a balm
of whispering silk, opening like altars . . .

The far room has a window on the sea.

Seasons

miracles

Winter has been long
and summer lost, like some vague garden, twice —
the real, then the remembered warmth has gone.
February.
Weeks of dark waking have covered over dawn.
Then
translucent wash of lavender brushed fresh
cross one whole morning corner of the sky!
     — God's sleight of hand
        is slower than the eye.

Spring's tramp carnival
has packed its stars. Our running feet stop.
What happened to the day of festival?
In spite of April,
branches stay dark and last year's grass stays dull.
Then
as though it has come down instead of up,
with one warm night of rain comes green!
     — The change of many days
        one day is seen.

Autumn hangs on,
windless and precious and golden brown,
held halfway in its rush from red to bronze.
Indian summer.
Like the room of love, present and round.
Then
one windy day has brought the leaves all down
and ended autumn, and pulled the trees apart!
     — A change of season,
        like a change of heart.

diary

November first
Today the leaves came down.
You see, I told you so.
Remember that red branch way back in August?
I told you then it all would come to this.
Just a matter of time.

But the cold gray
of bark and stone
was colored gray
when gold was gone.

January first
Today the Tree came down.
You see, the party's over.
They couldn't fool me with their balls and stars
I told you they'd be packed away again
and that would be the end.

But the dark hemlock after the sparkling tree,
the long lone walk after bright gaiety
is Winter found again
more than a Christmas lost.

inheriting winter

This spring of morning,
this satin of peach in the east
presenting black lace of branches,
this cobalt and ochre and mauve
swirled out along a sprawling sky,
these colors of Easter
in January —
Is this where the others always lived?

Blue jays and chickadees
ornament the tamarack,
rosing nerves of maple
echo the rising sun,
and the snow is a dream of rainbows.
I live here, too, now,
adopted child of earth.

january thaw

The rightful heir, returned
from exile, reigns.
Night breathes like my dog on the hearth,
and I know the names of the stars.

Snow in my woods, relaxed
to fragile lace, prestos
spring wildflowers in my heart, opens
pathways to forgotten summers.

The sky, robin's egg blue, loves me
unconditionally, the black December spruce
are lamps of gold. As though
I were forgiven, and had time.

march

The yellow crocus crow and yell
yes to the sun —
spread and sprung as spirits spell

    Presto! Spring has come!

        (But I'm wise
           to that cloud in the skies.)

Then the whizzing wizard shows
scowls and whirls —
while his blistering blizzard blows
howls and swirls

    Abracadabra! Winter's come!

        (But I know
           what's under the snow.)

The next day I caught them
perfectly composed —
the snow, part melted
beside
the flower, part closed.

may

Everything so blooming
and everything so green,
as though they were expecting
the coming of a queen!

Everything so blooming
on every blossom tree,
as though a queen were coming,
as though the queen were me

and we a prince and princess,
broken from the spell
of all our wicked witches,
in our castle come to dwell!

Everything so green
and the blooming not yet done,
summer is beginning,
but   not   quite   yet   begun.

So seasons ever bring
what years refuse us all,
to live again in spring
with all we know of fall.

june

This sudden garden
of greening and blooming,
of fluttering and flowering
careening and zooming —
draped by the prom-dressed trees,

this quick carnival
of lavender and yellow and rose
and blue and poppy and
green and green and green —
with a thrill of scarlet.

Swallowtail ballet with the wild iris,
tasseling of bent grass in fringe beside the brook,
beetle trapezing from blade to
blade, jigsaw bee, rush-hour ants,
trees sequined with birdsong.

These laughing clouds, sweet
ghosts of childhood skies, attend
this brief theater of passionate highways
that blooms all lifetime,
like a summer love.

let september come (ballade)

We float on warm, moist air. A summer haze
is softly in our hair, and on our eyes.
We stroll with southern ease like languorous slaves,
watching the moon move across the sky.
But in another room, red leaves stand by,
and clear reflections wait.
                              That crystal sun
needs cruel northern gales to make it rise . . .
Allow the storm, and let September come.

Somewhere, though far as France, those silver days —
distilled, rung from a perfect bell — still lie
as close as death, or dreams. Yet August stays,
and cannot find a way to go.
                         Say why,
when asters bloom, and when the wild geese fly,
do still the leaves stay green? Today I've swum
in summer's lake, yet autumn's brook is dry . . .
Allow the storm, and let September come.

When we were young, we did not see the ways
that August turns to fall, or recognize
the chance red leaf or branch that now betrays.
We did not see that, as the corn grow high,
the sun grows low.
                        But neither were we wise
enough to know that nothing is begun
but something ends — that gales, and all, pass by . . .
Allow the storm, and let September come.

My friend, when it is time that you and I
leave this season for another one,
and let something be born, or something die,
allow the storm, and let September come.

a song for november

October's leaves have fallen down,
the autumn sun is lower now,
the golden moon and month are done,
the harvest and the hunt are over now.

But acorns
are alive along our walks,
the sun comes
through the rhythm of the branches,
and berries
still stay blue on purple stalks . . .

And now the hills
have come again!
Though nothing lasts,
so nothing ends.

That gold and red
are in this gray,
not gone as I remembered . . .
The leaves may go
but we stay.
The evergreen
is ever green.

Glimpses

two roads

Two roads
go from my house
to your house . . .

a big one
that goes straight there,
and a little one
that winds along the coast beside the sea.

When I was young
I didn't have much time,
so I took the one
that went straight there.

Now I am old
I don't have much time,
so I will take the road
that winds along the coast beside the sea.

clear days

Clear days, by their perfection,
keep me a lifetime fool.
Being the exception,
they seem to be the rule.

red

A red maple tree,
knife of joy,
opens my red heart.

The red-winged blackbird
flies —
what was it I was sad about?

the bright side

If Santa Claus were not a lie,
we might not learn to give,
and if we didn't have to die,
we might not learn to live.

eureka

All life long
I've searched for the Truth —
philosophically
theologically
psychologically
meteorologically
illogically.

What makes things work
or not?
Will-power or grace,
free-will or fate,
God or the weather?

At last I've found It!
What makes things work is
to jiggle them.

the truth about roses

The rosebush,
has a hundred lush in fullest flower
flowing rushing growing gushing
in and over
creeping dangling leaping tangling
up and under
                                    and that is nature.

You
have polished a silver pot
and put three roses in it,
                            and that is art.

afloat but not adrift

Spring flows back under
my stranded boat . . .

letting me stop a book halfway,
not clean up my plate,
go to sleep by day,
leave early and come late.

distant harvest

He thinks
the apples he is gathering
are the fruit of summer.

He does not know
what other ripening they had
when only icicles hung on the branches.

the dog star

I have watched two dogs die
and I will watch this one.

And these trees have watched my mother die
and her mother before her,
and they will watch me.

And these hills will watch the trees die,
and those stars will watch the hills.

But I and my dog
watch stars
already dead.

souvenirs

A locket, a ring,
a carved bird with a broken wing —
a lucky stone
a pressed red maple leaf.

The water of the sea
has held their shape an hour,
the dew-jewels of dawn
have sparkled on their flower,
the lightning of the stars
has lit their tower.

Through them, like Christ,
the Kingdom crystallised
and once passed through the world.

habit

The Truth, as intellectual,
is pretty ineffectual
in coping with the daily grind,
or times of feeling glum.
Truth is not something that you find,
but something you become.

the source

We see the waves
we see the waving leaves,
but not the wind.

We see the shapes
we see their shadows too,
but not the light.

airport

Faceless strangers
delayed by storm
use rows of metal telephones
and get their faces back.

the chicken or the egg

When the sun comes out
The people come out
When the clouds begin
the people go in.

But once when I was sad
And the day was bad
I went out for a run
And out came the sun.

traitor

How quickly we embrace it all again —
the sap rising in our veins, the newborn world,
the singing colors of roadside flowers,
our lover's tryst with work,
the depths of those dear faces.

How quickly we embrace it all again,
unfaithful to the valley of pain and fear,
the way we used to drop our books
the last day of school,
and run toward summer.

recipe for enriched bread

To make bread
mix and knead the dough
           Feel it!

then let it rise
           See it!

then let it bake
           Smell it!

then take it out
           Eat it!

                      You will be full.

Fresh sweet wash flying

in the golden morning —

festival of flags.

puddles of petals . . .

the rho- do- den- drons

have gone too far.

yellow roadside flowers . . .
the same
as somewhere else some other summer,
as though
a season were a country.

Tomorrow he goes to the electric chair,
and tonight for his last supper he has ordered
steak, french fries, and cherry pie.

What will you order
the day before you die?

Raining flooding storming,
melting freezing,
snowing,
deer . . .

Sculptures patterns crystals,
shine and sparkle,
whiteness,
tracks.

For rest and recreation,
the T.V. stars, I think,
watch children doing homework
and housewives at the sink.

I lie down on my back
looking up —
the branches of the tamarind tree
are meandering highways
to the sky
in me . . .

Palm trees . . .
fountains of branches
hula-dancing in the wind,
raised among the stars . . .

His boyhood room
neat for the first time —
empty cocoon.

Gray-brown pastures of November,
ripe hunter's moon rising —
a song in our accustomed love.

The sailor in the gale
prays to God, but does not kneel
for his eye is on the sail
and his hand is on the wheel.

Happily Ever After

diamond

I had told you what it meant to me,
that board in the front of the church that said,
each week, since I was a child—
First Sunday in Advent,
Second Sunday in Advent,
Third Sunday in Advent,
and, at last, unbelievably, dizzyingly,
CHRISTMAS.
Because that was how it was,
finding you.

Now we were at our first midnight service
with the candles and the poinsettia
and the organ and the white banners, and
your shoulder close against mine.
You smiled at me, and nodded at the board,
"Christmas," you said.

We walked home that new Christmas Eve,
with the clean crunch of snow
under our feet,
and the Star of Bethlehem,
descended unto earth.

how i do love thee

I love you means that when you lie beside me
I am not cold in winter and when you sleep
I am not afraid in the wind.
and that you make noise when I am trying to think
and that I bring you coffee in bed
and that your smell on the pillow gives me peace.

I love you because you don't understand me sometimes
until later
and you explain Einstein to me as though I were
a whole classroom
and when I asked you to tell me the story of your life
you did.
And because sometimes you ignore me
but you know I am there.
I love you wanting us to go for a walk
when I am busy
and taking me off my path
to make new trails through the woods
and bringing us home a different way.

And it means that we have seen the same seas
and climbed the same mountains
but enough apart that
together
we have seen the world was round.

And if I were lost and sick in the night in a strange place
and called
you would come.

Sometimes lover
sometimes adversary
always another life to warm my own.

forgiveness

I didn't get the part. Someone else
was going to play my role.
Pushing it out the front door with anger:
It was all HIS fault.

But in the night finding it
seated at my table, slipped in by the back door,
my old Moriarty in sheep's clothing.
It was all MY fault.

You were awake too. Your old monster
had got in too.
We lay together and took each other in our arms
like children, telling, listening
opening our cupboards of black and slimy snakes
and our closets of vile corpses.

And, after all this show and tell,
we were both still there,
not gone in a puff of smoke.
A hero is a man only to his valet
and you would love me with a runny nose.

The next morning
I picked blueberries in the field
in the woods in the mountains
in the sun.
With no stage and no applause
but with, for the first time,
blueberries and the sun.

the way to the bridge

We had come one way
from the wilderness
through thirty miles of flooded trails
and washed out fords,
cold and sore
and longing for the sun.

They had come the other way
from the village
along two miles of broad woods road
and goldenrod,
dry and warm
and the day just begun.

They sat on the bridge
and heard the water flow
under the bridge.

We lay on the bridge
and heard the water flow
inside us.

time machine?

So, after two years,
I come back the day I left,
at the beginning of everything, in May.

I know the way, know
what is around this corner —
the shoemaker, the ice-cream factory ...
I know the way so well that

those two years,
all that new life on the farm with him
could just have been a dream ...
or would he, still there,
watch down the road for me,
wondering why I did not come home?

I know the way so well that
I can go up this path, around
this corner, over
this stone wall to
the field beside my house.
Here I can lie down under
my giant maples that
were the wilderness for me,
I can look up and
be lost, and found, again.

Then I could walk across
the field over
the driveway and up
the steps to
the door.

hunter's moon

Here alone
over the pastel dunes
the pale hunter's moon
comes cool and silent
like a goddess.

There with you over the red-gold hills
our orange harvest moon
rose round and laughing
like a pumpkin.

ghosts

When I am alone
    I hear the wind around the corner
    the radiator steaming
    the shutter banging
    the board creaking
    and think they are ghosts.

When I am with you
    I hear ghosts
        and think they are
            the wind around the corner
            the radiator steaming
            the shutter banging
            the board creaking.

remodeling

Our farm has an old house,
a barn, a carshed and a shack.
Being on a mountain,
with late and early frosts,
you might as well forget eggplant,
but you should see our broccoli.

Tomatoes do well
against the south wall of the shed —
not in the field, open to freeze
and northern wind.
But the field is good for corn —
the deer don't come there,
so near the road.

We talk about tearing down the shed —
it's getting old, and leaks a little.
I wonder where we'd dry the herbs and onions,
though, and store the feed and tools.
Then there's the back room — too cold
and dark for living in. Someday,
we say, we'll make it into one of those
new solar green houses. But now
the cabbage keeps all winter there still crisp,
and hams and bacon last a year or more.

We ought to insulate the roof, they say —
that way, we wouldn't have to live downstairs
half of the year, in just two rooms.
But, the way things are, upstairs is just right
for storing squash and beets,
and knowing a warm back under the covers.

It's the thing these days
to remodel old farms,
renovate relationships,
or move to Florida.
But we stay here with jays and chickadees,
sunbathe behind the barn,
go south beside our stove on snowy nights,
learn waiting with winter trees,
joy with the round of days,
and forgiveness with the rising of the sun.

the stowaways

I packed my toothbrush,
my towel and my hat;
I packed my nightshirt,
my T-shirt and my book —
but I didn't pack you,
and I didn't pack the moon.

I drove for a day on the turnpike,
I flew for a day on a big jet liner,
I travelled by taxi and by ferry and by jeep —
but you stayed home in our mountains,
and the moon stayed home in the sky.

I left forests and brooks,
and flew to turquoise seas —
I left hemlocks and snow
and sailed to coral sands . . .

— but, how did you get here,
you and the moon?

out of season

Two weeks before Christmas
the woods have opened like spring
and I can sit beside the brook.
The hemlock over there is gold
and my eyes can touch the oak.

Brown grass and asters
come close as green
and I lift my face to the sun.
Today I can remember summer.

No, not quite.
Not till you December stranger
come like June again
with eyes that make me beautiful
and ears that make me wise.

pastorale

You stood there, tall and white
in the clearing beside the brook,
your hair tousled like a boy's.
You stood there, a wild buck
belonging to the brook,
and invited me to come
as though it all belonged to you —
and it did.

So I came, shyly.
With my back to you
(as though to face the brook)
I unwrapped my dress,
and sat on the rock to bathe.
When I slid into the pool
the cool water covered me,
and I dared to look up
at you standing there —
betrayed.
Then I knew you had been watching,
and you knew I knew . . .
so you laughed, and splashed me.

Wherever did it go, our pastorale,
in all this clamor of things to do?
Whatever could we have done with it
in all this rummage of blunders and stumbles?

But it will open like the light of a violin
as though
in some foreign land a stranger spoke
the language of our home.

how to sail in one easy lesson

Of all things
he was trying to
sail
with a cracked mast.
the very thing that
holding everything
had to hold . . .

. . . the park beside my house
the Seine in Paris
the Mountain in Montreal
the beach in Annisquam
in the woods
a brook
in the room
a fire
on the table
a flower . . .

. . . in every country
a different place
with the same center.

Burnt toast / scorched collars / blown fuses
insomnia / sleepiness / snow / cold
trying to solve / trying to get done / trying
trying
trying to sail with a cracked mast!

Naked
we lie down together
and make whole
the center that heals us.

october snowstorm

Let's see this spring now
what they do,
if they send out new
branches, there where ones were split then.
You said they would, or might.
That gave us something to hang onto then.
People need that.

The evening news was like home video —
Our own queens of autumn
mugged at their coronation
and left to live like bagladies,
but ours still
to learn to love the best we could.
People do that.

So we began to prune and drag and pull
the mangled limbs — another fall, then,
we wouldn't get at our dream cabin on the hill.
But this was there to be done, and people do that.

Then, after awhile, we were laughing and
calling joyful insults to each other. The work healed us.
Work does that.

the sunflower

Today it is still there
waning
beside the picnic table.
It is there forgotten on the ground
upside down and inside out.
Or is it?

Yesterday at noon
she had been picking wildflowers.
"Fwowers," she had called them, smiling.
He had had the genius
to pick a sunflower for her
from his garden behind the house,
and bring it to her as though she were a queen,
as though it were the moon
and he her genii slave.
"Fwower!" he said, triumphantly.
"Fwower!" she had echoed with complete delight.

He gave her the world, better than it was,
the way a grandfather can.

the guest

I could
just
be quiet and listen,
let the bubbles of my mind
effervesce
in carefree globes.

I could
just
let you be my guide
in the woodland of your thoughts,
take off my shoes
and enter
the temple of your memories.

I could
drink
from the cup of your dreams.

pass words

Are we speaking, then,
so easily of it —
as though it were the weather?
Has that stranded moment
come afloat, then,
with the tide?
Where are the barricades, the moats,
the dug-in trenches?

My brambles and thickets
relax like grass,
your Maginot line
surrenders without a fight,
and the Red Sea parts indeed.

born again, and again

Like a newborn fawn,
moist, and shaky on its legs,
I stagger to my feet —
naked, without even my skin.

I babble drunk on bubbles,
snuzzle honeysuckle,
forget what I am saying,
and almost miss my train.

I feast on the clear taste of apples
and the veins of leaves.
I am the clouds,
and I tremble at your touch.

but these candles

Sometimes, I would light candles, and
you would put on music
and I would come into your arms —
You always said they were my home — and slowly
kiss the deep crease between your eyes.

And we would lie together within the circle
until our bodies, remembering,
would run and laugh like children coming back to summer,
down all their secret paths,
to all their glens

until they burst their skins, flooding
into each other.
We couldn't tell whose legs were whose,
we'd laugh and say, as
our candles and our music came back.

The doctor's office
Sorry I can't do more. Better get your affairs in order
my love, my love too fast too fast thanks, pal
quick, the pan the oxygen the phone
dear God let him swallow it
no better, friend
help me help me I'm here I'm here help me
I'm here
help.
The blank gaping of your vacant face.
The deep crease between your eyes turned to stone.

Now, morning after morning,
your pipe on the table has not moved,
not one tiny bit.
What am I to do with it?
What am I to do with these candles and this music?

the difference

I want to tell you about that brook,
the one that runs under the road
halfway up the hill.
I always stop there on my way back down
when I walk up to the blue mailbox,
the way we used to walk together.

I want to tell you how the brook
opens down, out of a mystery of woods —
you can't see where it comes from,
as though there'd always be another bend
if you tried to follow it to the source.
It's like a queen the way it moves in stillness.

I want to tell you how it settles out
in a pool beside the road,
and seems, almost, to rest.
There is a hemlock there, presiding, and rocks
and stalks of grass. But, from one corner of the pool,
a secret stream slips away under the road.

I want to tell you how, on the other side,
the brook shouts and tumbles down
like joyous children crowding out of school,
how the sunlight bumples it along
with flutes of song,
how the sky there smiles behind the trees.

★   ★   ★

It's snowed now.
More snow than we ever had.
I wished you could have seen it.
I wanted to tell you how high it piled,
how full and fresh it was the next day in the sun,
how the sky was perfect blue.

I still walk up the hill to the blue mailbox,
but the brook is frozen now
with thick ice, and buried under snow.
The snow banks are so high beside the road
you can't see over. Even if I stop to listen,
the way we used to do,

there is no sound.

if winter comes

That late patch of coltsfoot up the road
surprised me, all right.
Here it is almost the end of April, and somehow
I never thought to walk the other way,
down to the corner beside the dam
where those perky little suns
first push through the asphalt overnight.

They would be there like pirate's treasure
that first bright day in April.
I'd say to you, "I'll bet the coltsfoot
will be out today,"
and, sure enough, it would be.
And you'd say, "Well, how about that!"

So, it's gone ahead this year without me, has it?
Can it come back, then,
when you cannot come back?
The coltsfoot can,
but not the pirate's treasure.

departures

The shadbush was in bloom
when I came here to live with you.
We called it cherry then.
I am afraid that it will bloom again
this year, the way it always has.

I am afraid the forget-me-nots
you planted for me beside the door
will suddenly be there,
as though they did not know,

that the maples will celebrate
and the lilacs bear
their careless flowers
as though no one had told them.

I am afraid, then, that June
will keep on and on
with its old story of joy
until it turns my head,

that this ship of time
will draw away from the shore
where we lived together,
as I stand on the deck
straining my eyes to see.

love story

I wish sometimes our love story were a book
that I could remember again,
having forgotten just exactly how it went,
but knowing it was all there — all
the favorite parts, like "Lilac Weekend",
as you called it,
when I told you I didn't know what love was.

Now I know. I know it all.
I know it is sometimes not understanding,
but still staying there.
I know it is having you interfere with everything,
and make it all possible.
It is trying to show you how wrong you are and
wishing you wouldn't tap your foot and
being sure you have stolen my glasses
(as sure as you are I have stolen your pipe)
and wanting to tell you everything
funny or beautiful or divine.

And it is, when you are sick,
wanting to walk with you and sit with you and
fight for you like a lioness and
think of everything and not forget anything and

when you die
it is finding,
when the lilacs bloom again,
what you meant —
the way we only understand a book
when we have closed the cover.

his daylillies

So gold so lemon so peach so lifted up
as offerings above green fountains,
so agreeing with the breeze
so blessed with dew
so trumpeting,
as though
this one day's fullness
were some final triumph.

Beautiful more than ever,
this summer of all summers,
when he no more can come.
You, of all flowers,
my fellow souls, my sisters,
that needed him, to bloom.

So gold so wine so rose so company
that makes earth whole again, sweet key
to something so gold in me,
tell me your secret word
behind mind's smug back,
heart's sanity that brings the exile home.

chill draft

Summer's crowding clambering, things
tumbling one before after around over the
other, pushing in between, spreading into the
spaces busy busy, so much to do to grow to be
has slowed.
Squash lie ripe in the fields.

No, please, not yet —
he's not here anymore
with his warm back and his big voice,
his love of chocolate,
his anger at the world,
his wonder at a wasp's nest.

Ancient chant of crickets
enchants a truce of goldenrod,
constellations of asters
last.
But a telltale sun
is late all day.

Oh, sure, I know, I know, but —
so soon?
A single daylily remembers,
like a wandering flute.

tryst

It would be the time of goldenrod and asters,
blooming together between summer and frost
the way we did.
I would be lying here by the brook, here
in this secret clearing of ours.

You would come — not by the long path
through the field from the house —
you would come the other way,
down the hill from out of the woods
and across the little bridge.
You could do that and no one would know.
You could come to me out of the woods
out of your long absence.
And you would say, "Hello, Baby."

I would not ask any questions, and
I would not need to say
that last unsaid
"I love you"
that beats its wings against the glass of death.
Now I would have the time
of goldenrod and asters
to love you with this full and simple heart
that hangs ripe on the vine of grief.

physics lesson

One time my son, who is a physicist,
was explaining to me about
electrons and probability and all, and
after a while, I laughed and said that oh, yes,
I got it, because it was like the way
there was a high probability
you could be found
sitting in your chair in the living room.
"Well, sort of. But not exactly," my son said,
tolerantly. But he laughed, too.

For a year, maybe more, I kept
thinking maybe just once your electrons might
defy the high probability
you could not be found
anywhere.
I would check your chair in the living room,
just to be sure,
every morning
when I came downstairs,
or afternoons when I came home from town.

But I have found you when
I stopped
beside a stream the way you would,
or noticed
sawdust off the path
and looked up
to see a woodpecker's hole
I would have missed,
or when I drank a glass of water
slowly.

And yesterday I found you in
a book that made me hear
something you once said —
like that daylily you'd planted beside the door
that bloomed for the first time
last summer.

object lesson

Reaching in under the couch for
a pair of shoes I hadn't used for a while,
I found your old moccasin,
covered with the dust of a year.

I have searched the whole world round
and watched in our old places,
I have listened across the silence
and walked on our old pathways,
I have awakened in the night
to the echo of your hand on me.

Last winter you almost said, "Thanks, Pal,"
when I fed your chickadees.
Last spring you almost stopped with me
to stand beside our brook.
Last summer you almost took my hand
to do our evening walk.
And when I had a second cup of tea
beside our stove last fall
you were there
almost.

I have made pilgrimages
and played music and lit candles and put flowers.
I have searched the whole year round,
and found

an old moccasin
covered with the dust of a year.

secret passages

The first time I found you
it was by taking a trail in the woods
I had passed a hundred times,
but never taken.

And then I showed you a pool
in a corner of my lake
that had been my secret place,
and you made your camp there.

Through all our years, I kept
on finding you, across
the interstellar space between
your chair and mine,

when I took a trail in my heart
I had passed a hundred times,
but never taken,

when I showed you a place
in a corner of my soul,
and you made your camp there.

new friends

It's warm today, and soft
with a damp freshness, a gentle
melting in the woods — cues
of spring in January.
A year ago
it was cold and hard.
The snow piled high and there was no
sound of water running underneath.

Your friends
are, little by little,
becoming my friends,
shyly, oh so
carefully, not knowing just how
to behave without you between us
keeping us together,
and apart.

I begin to get the feel
of when to water your plants
without always using my moisture detector,
and how to turn them in the sun.
Your chickadees
have been coming back
to the feeder, now that I've
outwitted the squirrel.

Sometimes I walk slowly, and see for myself
now the red berries off the path
or the high woodpecker's hole.
And today I stood by the brook
a long time, until
I began to hear the sounds that come
after the others have left
to the one who stands still.

And then I stood some more.

that number has been disconnected

It happens slowly, behind your back,
while you are trying to get the furnace fixed
in the middle of winter
or holding a sick grandchild
or going to the cemetery with your brother
to put flowers on his wife's new grave.

It happens silently, when you look away,
while you are going for a walk with your daughter
or writing to an old friend
or going out on a cold night to look at the stars
because there is no moon and the sky has cleared.

There are no flowers, no hymns, no prayers,
no one calls to see how you are doing.
There is a notice in the mail
that your mortgage payment is late
your bad knee is acting up
and it's time to pack the car to go up to the lake.

And his sweet painful absence
that was your company
has slipped away,
taking even your tears.

the next lover

She has come out and danced in the waving meadows,
that girl in me who, though I age, dreams young,
whose heart goldens like alchemied barn windows
late afternoons in breaking slants of sun.

She has run hills and sailed the blue blue skies,
found her true north and sweet careening madness,
lain beside him, naked, her soft thighs
clasping his hard passion with all gladness.

That was her dream. But no next lover comes
to recognize me here and want to know
the way you did, and those deep other ones
who pressed their signatures upon my soul.

Let April come, the way it used to be
a life ago,
just spring and me.

once upon a time

Yes, once upon a time the summer stayed,
though winter came,
and once the violins and woodwinds played,
and Christmas came.
And once upon a time love songs were true
and earth was whole
and clouds could laugh and sky be all its blue,
and flowers unfold
full like those roses of childhood June.
Coach from a pumpkin and gown from tatters,
Once we lived happily ever after.

Questions

bitten moon

What, you too so diminished, moon?
weren't you full last night
and splendidly made whole, all
of a piece? Now look at you
collapsed, not even perfectly
concave — obviously
unachieved.

Did we shout "Victory!" too soon
then? Or did we shout too late?
Like the receding wave along
the sand, each break and surge
rolls under into waning — the breath
of minute or of month,
and my own breath.

But what if,
having waned the thousandth time
after the thousandth triumph won
By trial or error
or the grace of God,
you had not quite the heart
to wax again?

depending on which world you mean

Columbus proved the world was round
by sailing round it,
which, geographically, is sound —
for so I've found it.

The latest shape appears a pear
to erudition.
How could those ancients think it square?
By in-tuition.

Their simple way of thinking that
let us not scoff at,
for I can prove the world is flat
by falling off it.

where the lilacs are

I come to them
through winter and through waiting
slowly, across a field . . .

I come to them
to lavender and laughing
slowly, on naked feet . . .

But have I come too soon
or dreamt too long?
The scent is gone.

I came to them
the lilacs of my longing
where they seemed to be . . .

Then on another path another day
the scent of unseen lilacs
came to me.

the miracle

The pastor was fat.

Before he was saved he had been a rock singer
working for the devil.
Now he preached about sin and heaven and hell
and being saved or lost.
He said 'we' when he meant 'I'
and 'you' when he meant 'we',
and he made bad jokes.

He had a loud voice that rose and fell
saying God would bless us if
we came to church and
gave generously to the Lord when the plate was passed
and didn't smoke or drink or commit adultery,
And he had rings on his fat fingers.

He had a loud voice, but we couldn't hear him.
The babies cried, the children squirmed
the girls whispered, the boys smirked and slumped
and the adults sat straight with their arms crossed
staring at him attentively and thinking about Sunday dinner.

Today, though, he brought his guitar.
He stands in the pulpit and sings,
dares to sing
with his pure sure tenor voice

the voice of the thin pastor
singing what he could not say
that we are all both lost and saved.

self portrait

I just opened the door of my life
and it all came clattering down
around my head and all out over the floor
like Fibber McGee's closet —
the unanswered letters,
the unpaid bills,
the dusty corners,
the overflowing files,
the "things-to-do",
the things to be undone.

And somewhere out there, in the soft spring rain,
is a little boy in a red raincoat
on his way to see a certain great Cathedral
he has in mind.

not you

"Don't wait too long to come," you said,
"I'm getting a little long in the tooth."

But you were the one, of all of them, who didn't age.
But you were tall and brisk and wore tweed suits,
watched birds and cartoons and loved Chinese food.
You were the one, of all of them,
who lived in the country and walked with long strides
and came and went as you pleased.

"Don't wait too long to come," you said.
So even you plan to die.

Then does the clock indeed run down
does a life set like the sun,
when camping without a lantern I must stop
and go to sleep
what ever remains undone?
No way to hold to shout to push back
to say there must be some mistake
to say just one just one more minute
just one more thing I have to do
one more flower I have to see
one more touch of love
one more word
one look.

Dim and dimmer
no way to know which fades
my eyes or the light,
dim and dimmer
and then too dark to see.

Or do the eyes behind my eyes
become the light?

frontiers

It's too hard, I said,
to have to take up living again
where I left off as a child,
to have just the things themselves —
a cold, rainy day, a birthday morning,
the taste of cinnamon on my tongue,
a stuffy nose.
It's too hard, I said,
to have just the play,
no cast party.
You'll get used to it, he said.

It's too hard, I said,
to have to shift the pack high on my shoulders,
push on to uncharted clearings,
open my eyes in the dark —
or sometimes just to sit it out,
pace the floor, do crossword puzzles,
cry, or think of laughing at myself.
It's too hard, I said,
to be that kind of pioneer
in the west of my old habit-ridden heart.
You'll get used to it, he said.

It's too easy, I said,
too shimmering, too giddy —
how can I dare to lie awake all night,
like after making love,
and be this sweet, sweet singing —
to ride through my hometown
in this white coach?
It's too easy, I said,
without the little-girl-with-a-curl
and her black ritual with herself.
You'll get used to it, he said.

coming across my old wedding portrait

As though she were some abandoned
child of mine,
or some lost sister,
that stranger that I recognize
stands centered in her soul,
looking calmly out of huge dark eyes.

Her head is like a flower on a stem,
fragile, but sure —
more beautiful than I have ever been,
with veil arranged like clouds around her face,
tight bodice, flowing gown,
and flowers in her hands,
forever on the day before her life.
Straight like the sapling, not knowing yet
the gnarled compromises of trees,
not knowing yet that, at the very most,
the earth will only live a trillion years.

Brief angel from lost corridors
between the walls of dreams,
her light illuminates the weave of God.

my old child

Locked in the third floor bedroom
where we don't go anymore,
we cannot hear her ragings,
except at night sometimes,
when everything else is quiet.

We occupy our lives,
shrunken to the first two floors now —
after all, nobody's perfect
and there are only twenty-four hours in a day.
We bring her food on a tray
that we leave at the head of the stairs.

But she has witch's powers
that cannot be confined —
under her spell, I wake up wide at 3 A.M.,
eat the whole chocolate cake
and am still hungry,
find fault with everyone.

Sometimes I have glimpsed her,
watching me out that high window
with silent eyes,
unforgiving of my arthritic knee,
waiting for me to live the life she dreamed.

Answers

my old child — ii

When was it I first caught sight of you
watching me from that secret attic window,
waiting for me to finish
with trying to please all of the people all of the time
while walking all of the Appalachian Trail
from Maine to Georgia
and back?

When was it I first discovered you,
living there silently in my blood
for all these years,
waiting for me to stop
to taste a glass of water,
waiting for me to remember
your clear brown eyes?

You came to me in white and flowing robes,
a child goddess
walking before me with a lamp,
sounding your battle-cry from up ahead,
deaf to all my excuses.

But where the path is staggered
my staggering step might follow better
than your sure foot.
Come walk with me and keep me true,
but let me teach you crooked.
Beyond your Himalayas
is a grail you never dreamed of —
your old sand bucket, full of pretty stones.

traveling light

I'm traveling light —
just a pack on my back,
so my hands are free
and my head too.

It took trips and trips of traveling with trunks,
hatboxes, bandboxes, matchboxes, cigar-boxes,
soapboxes, suitcases, briefcases, longcases, in cases,
and packages of all sizes coming untied . . .

It took trips and trips to learn
how little I really need,
and how much I need that.

But at last I'm traveling light,
so my hands are free
and my head too —

and lady, you're traveling heavy,
the way I used to do,
so let me give you a hand —
I've got two.

nauset beach

I

The waves roll in, roll out forever,
and the dunes stand.
The beach goes on and out forever
beyond the land
to the sunrise from some Himalayan mountain
to new and shining loves across the sea
to summer and to steamships and to islands
to all the grand and smiling possibilities of me —
I am the dunes I am the endless sands
I am the rhythm of the ancient sea,
and so I run forever,
for an hour.

The waves roll in, roll out forever,
and the dunes stand.
The beach goes on and out forever
beyond the land
to other actors in the roles I played
to other blonde-haired girls that look like you
coming to school where other teachers wait,
to other little boys in sailor blue,
running to other arms . . .

II

But my heart turns, as shadows after noon,
and though the road goes on,
the way goes home.
The wind is at my back now,
the sun is on my face, the beach that was a path
is now a place.

nauset beach cont.

Up by the dunes
are layers of years, where a slope has fallen away,
and my painted desert,
subtle as unseen sunsets.

Along the sand
I find my outward track
crooked — I thought I was going straight.
I stop, look back.
I sit, making circles in my sand,
and these waves tell me timelessness,
like that high hush of trees.
I read the hieroglyphs of gulls —
they've shared the beach with me,
and laugh at sandpipers.

Down by the sea
I know the waves —
ever the same, never the same.
hear the rough incoming yang
and the sleek outgoing yin.
I pick up a pretty stone
because I like it,
and a flat stone,
for skipping.

Back at the beginning
I climb the dune,
and find — all over,
the blue beach pea in bloom!

It had been there before,
but not for me.

look, ma, no hands!

To go on stage without
the lines without
the blocking without
the character without
the plot,
and have that old nightmare
become a dream of flying . . .

to walk on board without
my trunk shipped ahead without
my passport and my shots in order without
my bills all paid without
my travelers checks,
and have that old nightmare
become a dream of floating . . .

to be a gypsy in my own kitchen,
an errant knight about my daily chores,
to purr in the sun
ready to pounce.

transubstantiation

The choreography of ritual
is not as the crow flies
but, as the contour of the land allows,
a strategy . . .

       a patience
       waiting in locks toward the upper lake
       beyond the rapids. . .
       a persistence
       dusty feet of Zuni dancers
       drumming desert rain. . .
       a falling off
       from windward course, to sailing north
       by sailing east and west. . .
       a pacing
       the slow haste, the mountain haste
       of learned stubborn-ness . . .

a strategy that seems to the spectator
a strange and sinuous pursuit of phantoms,
to the ordained
a channel through known peril
toward known pleasure.

He who breaks through
to the upper lake, the desert rain
the windward buoy, the wilderness,
not by the awkward thrust of chance
but by the choreography of ritual
breaks through, he

       breaks bread that's Body
       and pours wine that's Blood.

altars and fountains

An altar is a place of pilgrimage
come to from hope or hopelessness or just
from curiosity; for miracles
for exercise, as part of the guided tour
or by mistake. So all of us have been on pilgrimage,
and been more or less impressed
by the crutches and patches and such in great array
that had been left at the altar by those who
supposedly had been healed and gone away.

A dispensary's not something come to, but some time
come upon, whenever limping life
is propped and tattered life is patched.
An act and not an altar. A clinic or a shoe shop
or a cup of tea; a telephone
a single flower, a song. A minor vice
a compromise — a minor virtue. A prosaic
sort of fountain given or found. Altars
make whole, perhaps, dispensaries make do.

Crutches, like miracles, can make the crippled walk,
better, maybe . . .
And better may be
the winding upward track or windward wake
where crookedness was strategy for straight.

meaning

Since my unawaited twin
born nameless and a princess,
I have learned to wait for
the second birth of everything —for
the echo from the opposite hill, for
the widening circles around the splashed stone, for
the silence after music . . .

Until I could see my lover's twin
coming secretly to me
when my lover left my side.

Then I saw the bird fly free
the day my father died.

thanks giving

I give thanks for the air that holds me up
when I remember to spread my wings,
for the cold that warms me
when I remember to breathe it deeply,
for the breeze that lifts my boat
when I give up my blowing on the sails.

I give thanks for the thirst
that leads me to other fountains,
for the hunger that drives me to other food,
for the pain that is the gate to secret gardens
when I remember that it asks me a question.
I give thanks for the sunrise that always comes
when I remember to wait for morning.

And I give thanks for the flight of a bird,
the touch of a hand,
a flower in a vase, the sound of rain —
for all my earthly angels.

i am that i am that i am

I spoke with the voice of the guru
and told her the secret she had been dreaming
of sunrise in the Himalayas,
but when she followed the guru to the ashram,
I whispered with the sound of wind in the trees.

I sang in the song of the pastor
stepping forward with his guitar
leaving his sermon behind him on the pulpit,
but when the pastor preached,
I smiled in the sky outside the window.

I walked with the steps of her cat
coming to meet her busyness at his own pace
out of the ancient mystery of panthers,
but when she asked her name of the forest,
I answered in the radiance of water.

I am the diamonds in the morning grass,
the jewels in stones washed by the waves,
the golden windows in gray barns at sunset.

after the breakfast dishes

She'd never had a cedar chest before --
not of her own, but had not dreamt that that
would make a difference, and had forgotten it.
It was not, after all, a treasure chest.

After the breakfast and the breakfast dishes,
and on her way to make the beds, she thought
the nights were warmer now, and would stay warm,
chances were, what with the trees leafed out
(for she had learned that spring, for all its blooming,
never stays until that fixative
of gracious green -- which is a sign that we
will want its shade.)
                                  Today would be as good
a day as any to change the blanket on
his bed for a clean, ivory-colored one,
one of those blankets from the cedar chest
she'd taken from her great aunt's house after
she died last spring. The blankets and the chest
were new to her, though to her aunt they had
been old. So she took one out, folded and smooth,
and shook it out to spread across the sheet.

after the breakfast dishes cont.

        Ah! she shook more than she supposed --
        a world of rambling childhood summer,
        hot stones and wicker chairs, long closed
        by sprung-up thickets, brambles of
        thorned hopes and undergrowth of fears --
        lost castle of leaping into water,
        and of laughter lost a hundred years.

        She shook out that whole sloping shaded season
        of endless Eden ended (no -- covered over),
        in shaking out that known and unknown smell
        that at the gate of summer used to dwell,
        welcoming her to hollyhocks.

After the breakfast and the breakfast dishes,
found what she never sought, and could not find
by sorcery of soul or will of mind.

It was then, after all, a treasure chest.

a fool's paradise

I was always one
to stick to the trails, I was —
to get there and back,
to come the same way home.

Yessir,
I started what I finished, I did —
met things head on,
said what I meant and meant what I said,
took the bull by the horns
in the china shop,
and always cleaned my plate.
Yup,
I was nobody's fool.

Now, though, I'm my own fool.
I might even leave a book unfinished,
my plate half full,
change my mind, or go to sleep at noon.
I brake for sunsets,
find lucky stones and four-leaf clovers,
eat fruit in season,
fly in below the radar.

I see ultra-violet, infrared,
diamonds in the morning grass,
and cobwebs in the woods.
I get FM,
shortwave,
signals from outer space,
and, beneath your words
sometimes,
the subtitles of the heart.

something more

The real wine
bubbles up like springs
out of humdrum and sadness,
comes up like scents
now, in the clear air,
like scents
from rainy afternoons,
from the virtue of having done my income tax,
from the flying fun
of playing childhood games
for grown-up stakes,
like springs, like scents from the sweet bed of night,
the field of morning.

The real wine
floods sometimes like a tide
that floats me up,
comes into me like warmth,
tingles to my toes, my fingers
like warmth, like tides
like light, like light of spring,
like springs, like scents —
and yet not these,
but something more
that these are like.

what if she forgot to leave her glass slipper?

She would never in her wildest dreams
have thought up this scenario.
Yet here she was — coach, footmen, etc.
and, as it turned out, quite
equal to the occasion.
She had to be of royal blood,
somewhere way back.

Glass slippers must be high tech orthopedics,
for here she was, bunions, hammertoes and all,
waltzing past wallflowers with the prince.
This sparkling spinning world
had been just waiting for her entrance.

The next day —
an empty doorstep,
a mute telephone,
her heart at half mast,
and all these damn ashes to be swept.

Cont. ⟶

what if she forgot to leave her glass slipper cont.

But tomorrow,
dawn's subtle gray will seep
between your windows,
under the curtains of your eyes,
and, tomorrow,
when you open the door of morning,
a bird will fly down to the tamarack tree
and your valley will be a well of freshness.

Cool air warms your cheeks
and, beneath its brilliant architecture of ice,
the stream
is the secret presence of summer.
There is music, and
you are the violin.
You are still here,
and the morning is for you.

how to break a spell

Never again would there be
her sixteenth birthday ball.
And she was so beautiful,
so very much loved.

The king and the queen made ready
the most wonderful feast
that could be imagined,
and ordered the finest wines.

They garlanded the great hall
with the most flowering flowers,
and commanded the most musical musicians
to play her favorite songs.

They went over and over the guest list
making sure to invite all of the good fairies,
and none of the bad ones,
and they locked the doors and sealed the cracks,
just in case.

But neither the king, who was too careful,
nor the queen, who was too carefree,
remembered to lock the window,
and that is, of course, where the bad fairy came in.

Cont. ⟶

how to break a spell cont.

She would never miss a party.
The last time, they had remembered to lock the window,
but forgotten to lock the door.
That's the way she works.

"She keeps coming back," said the king,
"no matter what we do."
"She is very dedicated," said the queen.
"Maybe she isn't all bad."

"That's possible," said the king.
"Could be she's trying to tell us something."
"It might be easier," said the queen,
"to learn to live with her."

So they welcomed the bad fairy royally,
and kissed her on both cheeks.
They made her guest of honor loyally,
and sat her at the feast.

She turned into the life of the party,
and they, spell-broke, appeared
the princess and the prince they used to be
asleep a hundred years.

the hills and the path (sestina)

When I came back the summer I was big,
I found again the rhythm of my hills
seen from the lake — all over all,
as easily as Indians I would go,
and never crack a twig! Oh, I would walk
as pure as pioneers along my path!

The whole woods would be my path —
my strongness and my stride would be as big
as my desire! From dawn to night I'd walk
as fast as light, and the rhythm of the hills
would be my pace! Ah, now at last I'd go
and never stop or turn again at all!

But there were goldenrod along my walk,
and flocks of golden grosbeak arriving all
suddenly, and sunset like autumn on the hills.
There was the fawn standing in my path,
watching me as I watched it. There were the big
hemlocks and the brooks, wherever I would go.

And there was underbrush, and brambles all
the way, and many times I lost the path —
washouts and downed trees I had to go
around, and cliffs that were too big
for me to climb — and night came in the hills,
and wind, and stones and stumbling broke my walk.

Cont.

the hills and the path (sestina) cont.

I have gone longer than I have left to go,
but not as far. There is not time to walk
the way of Indians — it is too big.
There was not ever time to walk it all.
Now I see the end of my path,
and now I see the endlessness of hills.

Only a few, then, among so many hills
seen from the lake? Why did I not go?
So many sudden monsters on the path,
so many hidden flowers on my walk,
not seen from the lake. Once and for all,
I shall not save the world. I am not big.

Only eyes are big as light and as the hills.
But I know all when knowingly I go,
and when I walk for walking, tread every path.

afterlife

As I was saying,
these stark branches against the sky
have their own beauty. They suit my mood.
One gets used to winter, don't you think?
It's more in keeping with the way things are.

Wait a second now — what's with this
russet halo on the maples?
Was it there yesterday?
But what about my bare branches?
A flagrant purple crocus answers me.

So now it all begins again,
the girls in white with flowers in their arms,
the laughing clouds, the smell of fresh-mowed grass,
the mountaintops, the streams, the fields, the stars,
the bare feet in the sand, the open paths.

In spite of everything?
The Nobel Prize that I can never win
the Moby Dick that I can never write
the Appalachian trail that I can never walk
the hundred children I can never have
the old home sold
the clearing overgrown
the road closed.
And those dear kidnapped faces,
amputated limbs of my heart,
in spite of them?

But this sweet warmth of earth
this childhood smell of grass
this clear taste of melon after fast.

mary and martha

Mary is the summer the south the soul in me,
the child who can hear heaven
and who loves the golden leaves —

    Martha calls her in from play.

Mary is the singer the singing and the song
the dancer and the dancing
and the dance the whole day long —

    Martha makes her take a bath.

Mary is the tall wind, hushing high apart,
and the warm wandering woods
and the deep stream at its heart —

    Martha picks up after her.

    But Martha's windows washed
    both eyes and soul,
    and Martha's hearthfires warmed
    and made us whole

as Mary's tears have washed
and laughter burst —

So may we live in heaven
    and on earth.

how to shovel the walk

I meant to shovel the walk
or shovel for an hour
whichever got done first.

But the walk was hard
and the hour was slow
until I stopped shoveling the walk
and started to shovel the snow . . .

Then the shovel was my drummer
and the trees and sky my strings
and the snow was my dancer
and the dancing was my wings.

So the shovel and the snow and I
made love all the day,
and the walk and the hour —
well, they must have gone away.

But they came back shoveled,
when we had done with shoveling.

all natural

Love is an aphrodisiac,
sleep drugs the insomniac,
pain is an anaesthetic,
water is dietetic.
Bubbles make us burp,
soup makes us slurp,
work improves the heart,
gas makes us fart.
Pollen sets us sneezing,
shivers stop us freezing,
heat makes us sweat,
shock makes us forget,
sorrow makes us cry,
and life makes us high.

the intruder

For years now
I've seemed almost to hear sometimes
this feeble crying off and on —
like that neighbor's cat
trapped down cellar after the blizzard.

"My imagination is playing tricks,"
I've said, for years now,
pulling my T.V. commercials tighter
around my shoulders.

But now, there it is again —
that feeble crying from down cellar.
What if, after all, there really were
something there?
When I open the door, it creeps out,
pale and eyeless
from living in the dark.

"All right," I sigh, "Let's hear it then."
It sits there like a sphinx until,
turning its head once, as though
I were to follow, it slowly moves away
into the priestly subculture of cats
that weaves within our world
its silver, silent thread.

the intruder cont.

> I follow, through ancient jungles in the meadow
> and secret passageways across the lawn.
> I learn to listen, to watch,
> to be ready to pounce, to sit still.
> I begin to remember my soundless native tongue —
> the same that pulls the tides
> and makes the leaves unfold,
> or fall.
>
> And I ride on his shoulders now —
> my pale eyeless cat,
> become a tawny panther
> with the eyes of God.

just say yes

I used to be afraid of fear.
I'd run, like prey,
but then I learned to stand my ground
and just turn away
by turning toward this sungold branch,
this friend's old need,
this hill to climb, these dishes to wash,
this tough grass to weed.

I used to think in storm or war
there can't be peace,
but then I found down deep inside
that out of the wind place
where I can bask on sunny shelves
with cat's sure art,
ready to pounce or run or fight
and live, with whole heart.

clearings

There is a garden
where raindrops of birds' song
sing in your veins
and flowers are sisters.

There is a house
where you can ghost through walls
from tomboy's trees
to Paris and amour.

There is a ship
with charts of your heart's seas
sailing
to your lost sanctuaries.

There is a trail
through underbrush of years
opening
to your old mountaintops.

There is a place
where your worn crippled soul
hammocks in silk
and mirrors melt to windows.

town and mountains

Once
I was in the town
and saw, beyond, the mountains . . .

then
I was here, with you,
and we were in the mountains . . .

and then
I was with myself
and the mountains were in me . . .

so when
the mountains come to the town,
I will go to them —
for I will know them.

the girl in the white robe

She sits in the center
among the brown grasses
under the blue sky.
On one side the blue brook flows,
on the other the blue sea comes and goes.
Above, a blue bird rests on the wind,
and the wind caresses the grass.

The brown arms of a tree
curve around her head,
letting a brown leaf fall across her face.
A brown butterfly flowers at her feet,
and a blue flower flies.
The wind caresses her brown hair
and her clear eyes are blue.

She comes to me out of the golden woods
and takes my hand.
She brings the smell of leaf mold
and the damp of moss.
She leads me in the sun
among the trees
beside the pools of water.

She brings me silence,
the wind in my hair,
and days like fountains.
She brings me morning
and sunrise on the river of the night.

The Last Word

You that loved me and that I loved
lose nothing

because
— more than anything, I think —
I have wanted to give you
yourself —
so from now on
you can take my place in your life,

because
the things you have given me
have been my greatest gift
to you,

because
we are together
the way we have always been
when we were apart,

and because
I have loved a lot of things you know —
maybe, more than any other,
the wind in the trees —
or maybe the sound of water in the woods,
or maybe one flower —
but you would know.
Look for me there

because
I am
all that I have loved,
as though
love were the verb toward every noun.